"*The Man-Eating Sofa* [...] patheti-cally written for school [...] dults to gain a better understan [...] e of the aims of the National Autism Strategy (June 2021). Whilst light-hearted and filled with humour, it does not detract from the seriousness of autism as a neurodevelopmental condition."

Karin Twiss,
*Senior Educational Psychologist and
Strategic Lead for Autism and
Neurodevelopmental Conditions*

"Plum Hutton makes the learning process dynamic, and understood within a real context, using a delightful story that children (8–12 years) and families will enjoy. The first parts of the story reflect the 'too frequent' and unnecessary challenges that many autistic children and their families will likely have experienced before gaining the necessary support and understanding. The story is positive and upbeat, and the experience of reading it . . . promotes the compassion, understanding, thought and optimism that are such key ingredients for supporting and embracing neurodiversity."

Caro Strover,
Educational Psychologist

"The book has a really engaging and strong storyline with brilliantly fleshed-out characters and gets across the confusion and frustration and the sheer 'thinking differently' of autism so well, as well as the wider struggles for the family. I especially enjoyed Lara's excitement at building her sofa – and then the testing out of the sofa by the teachers, which I had to read three times as I was laughing so much.

I can't tell you how helpful your book and guide have been in making the behaviour of autistic friends and colleagues so much more explicable to me and for providing such clear direction for improving the ways in which I can communicate with them too."

Elizabeth Ord,
Parent

The Man-Eating Sofa

People often say that 'school is the best time of your life', but for Lara, school is loud and confusing. She much prefers watching James Bond films or building furniture in her dad's workshop. When the teachers at Lara's new school realise that she is autistic, they are able to help with strategies to make school more tolerable for her. All except Mr Prender-ghastly. The headteacher has been looking for a way to gently direct Mr Prendergast towards a change of career, but it is Lara and her special man-eating sofa who finally help rid the school of the fearsome teacher.

This entertaining story, suitable for readers aged 8–12, explores some of the challenges faced by autistic pupils and those with social communication and interaction difficulties in mainstream schools. It highlights the stress and anxiety that young people with sensory processing and social interaction difficulties may feel in the noisy and unpredictable school environment, and identifies strategies that can be used to support them.

Also available as a set with a supporting guide, this book operates as a fun and engaging stand-alone story, both for children who are autistic themselves and those who are not. It is a must-have book for every classroom.

Plum Hutton is a chartered educational psychologist and former learning support teacher. She holds a doctorate in educational psychology. She has more than 15 years of experience working as a local authority educational psychologist and latterly has transferred to independent practice. Through her work she has pursued and delivered training on many areas of professional interest, including supporting children with persistent anxiety, attachment difficulties, literacy difficulties and sensory processing differences.

Plum is a keen storyteller. She has gathered inspiration for her writing from her work, the challenges of parenthood and also through a nomadic existence as an Army wife, which has taken her to many locations across the UK and as far afield as East Africa.

Adventures with Diversity

**An Adventure with Autism and Social
Communication Difficulties:
The Man-Eating Sofa Storybook and Guidebook**
The Man-Eating Sofa: An Adventure with
Autism and Social Communication Difficulties
Supporting Autism and Social Communication
Difficulties in Mainstream Schools:
A Guidebook for *The Man-Eating Sofa*

**An Adventure with Dyslexia and Literacy Difficulties:
A Nasty Dose of the Yawns Storybook and Guidebook**
A Nasty Dose of the Yawns: An Adventure with
Dyslexia and Literacy Difficulties
Supporting Dyslexia and Literacy Difficulties in Schools:
A Guidebook for *A Nasty Dose of the Yawns*

**An Adventure with Childhood Obesity:
Down Mount Kenya on a Tea Tray Storybook
and Guidebook**
Down Mount Kenya on a Tea Tray: An Adventure with
Childhood Obesity
Supporting Childhood Obesity in Schools:
A Guidebook for *Down Mount Kenya on a Tea Tray*

The Man-Eating Sofa

An Adventure with Autism and Social Communication Difficulties

Plum Hutton

Illustrated by Freddie Hodge

Routledge
Taylor & Francis Group

LONDON AND NEW YORK

Cover image: Freddie Hodge

First published 2022
by Routledge
2 Park Square, Milton Park, Abingdon, Oxon OX14 4RN

and by Routledge
605 Third Avenue, New York, NY 10158

Routledge is an imprint of the Taylor & Francis Group, an informa business

British Library Cataloguing-in-Publication Data
A catalogue record for this book is available from the British Library

Library of Congress Cataloging-in-Publication Data
A catalog record has been requested for this book

ISBN: 978-1-032-07634-8 (pbk)
ISBN: 978-1-003-20804-4 (ebk)

DOI: 10.4324/9781003208044

Typeset in Helvetica
by Deanta Global Publishing Services, Chennai, India

To Bumble

Contents

Acknowledgements

I would like to extend my thanks to:

Iona and Ramsay Hutton for their encouragement and youthful perspective.

Claire Anson, Debbie Riall, Karin Twiss and Elizabeth Ord for their support and advice.

Alex Hutton for his patience, optimism and support during the writing of this book.

A Timeline of Lara's Life

Reception	Lara joins her first primary school.
Year 1 Year 2	Lara adjusts to school life and the school tries to support her, but it is a difficult time.
Year 3	Lara is diagnosed with autism.
Year 4	At the end of Year 4, Lara is involved in an incident at a museum and it is suggested that she needs a fresh start at a new school.
Year 5	Lara moves to a new school and Mrs Bingle's class, where she settles in well.
Year 6	Mrs Bingle prepares Lara for transfer to Kingscott Secondary School.
Year 7	• Lara transfers to Kingscott but leaves after a few weeks due to being terrified by the fire alarm. • Lara is educated at home from October to Easter of Year 7 and works on a carpentry project with her father. • Lara starts at Highfield Secondary School at the start of the summer term. • Most of the action in the story takes place during the summer term of Year 7.
Year 8	Lara continues at Highfield School.
Year 9	• Lara and her team enter into The Product Designers in Schools Award. • Mr Harris receives a surprising letter from Mr Prendergast.

DOI: 10.4324/9781003208044-1

Chapter One

In her twelve-year-old mind, Lara Frost divided the population into two groups – old people, which included everyone over the age of eighteen, and young people, which included everyone else. She had done this for many years and felt that the system worked quite well, although her mother often told her that adults didn't like being called old. Lara thought this was strange because adults obviously were old, so what was the problem in saying so? Lara wasn't very good at telling people apart, so grouping them all together made life easier. As a result of her system, there were a lot of 'old people' in Lara's life – her parents, teachers, aunts, grandparents and so on. Even some of her cousins had recently become old, when they left college and began wearing suits to go to work.

Lara thought that old people often said peculiar things. Come to think of it, young people often said strange things as well, but old people talked as though their words were important and that young people should take notice of them. One of the most ridiculous things that old people did was to talk fondly about school. Lara was often told by various well-meaning aunts and grandparents that "School is the best time of your life". This made her feel heavy and grey. When she thought back over her experiences so far, she decided that if school was as good as life was going to get, then life wasn't going to be much fun.

DOI: 10.4324/9781003208044-2

The first day of primary school was clearly etched on Lara's mind. It was a chaos of sensations, overpowering noises and smells. Her new uniform scratched her legs, faces peered at her – people chattering, laughing and stroking her hair. There were so many people. They kept asking her questions. She couldn't put a name to the emotion at the time, but her skin became hot and her heart thrashed against her ribs. She didn't consciously decide to run away; it just happened. One minute Bobby Dishford's big, toothy grin was in her face. The next minute, he was lying on his back with the breath knocked out of his lungs and a large purple bruise forming on his cheekbone. Lara had gone.

She remembered the cool wind on her face, the peace of the gentle outside noises, the space and blissful solitude. She was free, with her thumping heart and spindly legs powering her on across the playing field away from the Reception Class building.

She didn't hear the old person calling to her colleague, "Susan! Quick! She's done a runner!"

"Who has? Hang on . . . someone's thumped Bobby," replied another old person from the classroom.

"It's all right. I'll go after her," the first old person had called back, setting off after the rapidly disappearing figure who had nearly reached the wood on the edge of the school grounds. This particular old person was not well suited to giving chase to speedy four-year-olds. Her reading glasses, which were balanced on her head, bounced on her grey curls as she lumbered across the wet grass. Consequently, Lara was left undisturbed for some time, nestled under the branches of a large snowberry bush. Inside the bush, it was cool and dark and smelt of damp earth. Lara sat with her arms wrapped around her knees, gently rocking, listening to her breathing as it gradually slowed. There was no need to think, no need to talk, no need to try to understand. She felt safe in her own world.

Cocooned under the bush, it was a while before she became aware of a ragged wheezing and thud of heavy feet stumbling about in the undergrowth. An old person was muttering to herself.

"Oh! Good Lord!" Puff, puff. "It's only the first day of term," gasped the voice in a long breathless wheeze. "I really should have retired. I'm sure that running laps of the school grounds isn't in my job description . . . Ow! Blast!" Then in a louder more positive voice, "Lara? It's Mrs Jones. Are you there? Lara . . ."

The voice and the heavy feet crunched further away through the debris of fallen sticks. Lara let her mind return to her breathing, which was now slow and steady. Sucking air in . . . wait . . . puffing it out . . . wait . . . sucking in . . . wait . . . and out . . .

"Lara love. I know you're there. I can see your feet." Lara opened her eyes and saw a large bosom in a frilly blouse, one arm and half of an old person's face peering under the snowberry leaves. "Lara, please come out. It's all muddy under there. We can sit in the sun together for a bit." There was a long pause, and the eye peering under the bush blinked several times.

Slowly, Lara swung forward on to her knees and wriggled out from under the bush. She found herself standing in front of an old person who was leaning on her elbows with her bottom in the air. The teacher cautiously pushed herself up on to her haunches and retrieved her reading glasses that were hanging on the bush. She was still breathing heavily.

"You've got mud on your arms," stated Lara.

"So I have." The old person brushed the worst of the earth from her forearms.

"And on your shirt."

"Yes. It will need a wash when I get home."

"There are twigs in your hair."

"Are there? Can you take them out for me?" Lara frowned, staring at the old person's hair and imagining what it would feel like to touch. Eventually, she stepped forward and delicately removed two small sticks that had lodged in the teacher's hair.

"All done?"

Lara nodded.

"Right. Let's sit in the sun."

The old person heaved herself to her feet, brushing dead leaves and earth from her knees, and led the way back on to the playing field. There was a sturdy wooden bench near the edge of the grass, and the old person walked over and sat on one end, leaning back against the warm wooden slats and turning her face to the sun. Lara wriggled up on to the other end of the bench and sat with her legs dangling as they were too short to reach the ground. A blackbird began to trill in a nearby treetop.

In the distance, a teacher emerged from the Reception Class building and peered across the playing field, scanning the scene. She stopped when she saw the figures on the bench and raised an arm in greeting. The old person next to Lara raised her muddy arm in a friendly wave.

"That's Miss Beech, checking that we're OK," said the old person. Lara did not respond. They both sat in the sun staring at the school for a while until the old person broke the silence.

"School can feel noisy and confusing on your first day." Lara did not comment, but she was glad that the old person hadn't asked her a question. Old people asked too many questions. She was also glad that they were both looking at the school. It was often easier to talk when old people weren't staring at you.

"Some children feel scared when they start school. In fact, it's normal to feel nervous. It becomes easier when you get used to it."

On that first day, Lara couldn't imagine ever getting used to the sensational chaos of school – and in many ways she never did. She spent quite a lot of time under the snowberry bush in her first term. By November, the old people had persuaded Lara to calm down sitting on the bench, rather than by hiding under the bush, which was a great relief to the old people who had creaky knees.

Although the idea of playing with other children had appealed to Lara on one level, she had found them noisy and unpredictable. Often they sat too close to her and took her toys, or began playing in a way that was totally different from how Lara had planned. They didn't seem to understand why this was a problem for Lara, and it was so hard for her to explain. In her frustration, Lara had often screamed or pushed the children away and she hadn't understood why this was a problem for them. After a while, the other children stopped trying to play with her, and she decided that it was better to play on her own.

During those first terms of her early school life, Lara's parents, Mr and Mrs Frost, spent a lot of time in meetings with the headteacher – but not as much time as Lara had spent sitting on the bench.

Chapter Two

As time went on, Lara started to adjust to school life, but unexpected problems often cropped up, such as her fear of bears. When she was very young, her father had read her a poem about bears coming to eat people if they trod on the lines of the pavement, and ever since it had been a ritual for Lara to avoid the lines. This habit was not always easy to follow; it meant that walking down cobbled streets was very difficult, particularly when her feet began growing larger than the cobbles.

There had been a terrible scene on a school trip when the class arrived at a museum to find that it had a beautiful mosaic floor; there were intricate pictures created from tiny squares of stone. Looking at the floor and all the people walking on it made Lara feel as though her world was disintegrating. It wasn't possible to follow her rules; with every step, her classmates were walking on dozens of lines, which would cause them to be eaten by bears. There was no sign of any bears, but she knew that the bears must be there waiting to pounce because that was what happened when people walked on the lines. She couldn't walk on the lines. She couldn't explain to the other children about the bears. She couldn't hear what the old people were saying to her – there were too many lines and children and bears – and yet no bears. As the panic mounted inside her, she shrieked, desperately running through the

    DOI: 10.4324/9781003208044-3

crowds, trying to push her classmates, teachers, elderly ladies and even a woman with a pram off the mosaic and on to the safety of the flagstones at the edge of the room. As the befuddled visitors could not comprehend what Lara was trying to do when she pushed them aside, they instantly wandered back on to the mosaic. Lara became increasingly hysterical, dashing from side to side, trying to save everyone, with her teachers chasing behind her. The scene ended abruptly when she cannoned into a frail gentleman with a walking stick. He crashed to the ground with a crunch. Lara's feet left the floor as a security guard scooped her up under his beefy arm and carried her towards the exit.

Lara and an old person spent the rest of the trip sitting on a bench in the rain outside the museum. It was a comfortable bench but Lara noticed how the rain made the old person's hair stick to her forehead and how it dripped off her shiny nose. The old person was very quiet that day. While they waited on the bench, an ambulance arrived, its blue lights shining on the puddles. Lara watched the paramedics disappear into the museum and later emerge again wheeling the old man on a trolley. His face had a green tinge, but his eyes were bright, and he spotted Lara sitting silently on the bench beside the bedraggled teaching assistant. He spoke to the paramedic who glanced towards Lara and then came over to her.

"Mr Johnson would like to talk to you," the paramedic said to Lara.

"Are you sure that's a good idea?" the teaching assistant asked anxiously, flashing her eyes in Lara's direction.

"He said he wouldn't take 'No' for an answer," replied the paramedic.

"Come on, then," said the teaching assistant, standing up and shaking the rain off her skirt. Lara followed warily towards the wrinkly man. He seemed to be strapped to the trolley as if he might try to escape, and his glasses were a bit wonky. He looked at her with wise eyes.

"I'm so sorry for Lara's behaviour," began the teaching assistant.

"It was a bit surprising," the old man replied with a lopsided smile. The teaching assistant pushed Lara forward.

"Say sorry to Mr Johnson, Lara," she commanded.

"I'm sorry. I'm sorry. I'm sorry," Lara responded automatically. Mr Johnson noted Lara's blank face and rain-soaked hair.

"Lara," he said gently, "I need to know. What frightened you in the museum?"

Lara paused before she answered. She was calm now, but it still seemed hard to explain. "It was the bears and the lines and the squares," she replied.

A slow smile spread across Mr Johnson's aged face.

"It's the poem 'Lines and Squares' by A.A. Milne. One of my favourites," he explained to the teaching assistant. "It's about bears who wait on street corners to eat silly people who walk on the lines in the pavement." Lara nodded.

"Everyone was walking on the lines," she explained. "I had to stop them from being eaten."

"Yes, I see that now. You were trying to be helpful."

Lara nodded again.

"I knew there would be a reason for all that running around," said Mr Johnson. "There is always a reason, but often we grown-ups don't realise what it is."

"I hope you're not badly injured," said the teaching assistant.

"Just a bump on the hip," he replied. "I'm sure it will mend." He turned back to Lara.

"Lara, that poem is just a story. It is not true. There are no bears waiting to eat people who walk on the lines." Lara looked doubtful. Really old people could be forgetful or have poor eyesight. Maybe he just hadn't noticed the bears recently.

"Look at the evidence," he persisted. "My wife and I and all our friends have been walking on lines for over eighty years and we have never been attacked by a bear." Lara thought about this for a while.

"Perhaps they only eat young people. Old people might not taste nice."

Mr Johnson laughed. "They don't eat people, because they don't exist. They are not real," he said firmly. "You remember that. Now, if you will excuse me, I have an appointment with an X-ray machine. Goodbye." The paramedics began to wheel him away, and Lara watched, fixing all the contours of his face in her mind.

"Goodbye, Mr Johnson," called the teaching assistant. "I'm so sorry about your hip." He raised a hand in acknowledgement.

Soon after the trip to the museum, the old person in charge of Lara's school suggested that it would be best if Lara moved to a different school, for a 'fresh start'.

Initially, Lara hadn't enjoyed the 'fresh start'. It still had all the challenges of school but with different teachers, different children and a uniform that was uncomfortable in a different way. But that was before she got to know her new teacher, Mrs Bingle.

Mrs Bingle's class was an oasis of calm and cheerful good humour. She took everything in her stride and was no more daunted by Lara's ways than she had been by the day when rain began to pour through the ceiling of the classroom. On 'The Day of the Hole in the Roof', as it became known, lessons were learnt about teamwork as the children cleared all the resources away from the flood. They learnt about gravity and observed how water always flowed downhill, helpfully running away down the steps and out into the playground. They learnt about volume and how the large, flat baking trays from the kitchen were the best at catching the rainwater. Most of all, Lara learnt that she could cope when something unexpected happened.

Nature always seemed to creep into Mrs Bingle's classroom in the form of wildflowers arranged in a jar on her desk, newly hatched chicks or wriggling larvae that they fed on cabbage leaves until they transformed into butterflies. Lara's favourite times were sunny Friday mornings, when Mr and Mrs Bingle would arrive at school like Pied Pipers, with a string of hand-reared lambs trotting behind them. These were the orphan lambs from Mr Bingle's farm that could not be cared for by their mothers, and the children were allowed to feed them warm, frothy milk from a wine bottle with a teat over the end. After feeding time, Mr Bingle would collect the empty bottles and return to the farm with the round-bellied lambs skipping in his wake.

Lara blossomed in Mrs Bingle's unflustered, dependable care. Mrs Bingle could resolve a playground argument by simply raising one eyebrow. Mrs Bingle could understand Lara just by observing the set of her shoulders or the frown that creased her brow. Lara's mother said that Mrs Bingle was an angel, which was confusing because Lara knew that angels dressed in white, glittery robes, whereas Mrs Bingle wore flowery dresses and stout shoes.

When the time approached for Lara to leave primary school, Mrs Bingle planned Lara's transfer to Kingscott Secondary School with great care. Mrs Bingle was aware that moving from the security of her classroom to a bustling secondary school, packed with nearly a thousand teenagers, was going to be a massive challenge for Lara. Having a different teacher for each subject would mean that every lesson was unpredictable – in a different room with teachers who had different styles and different expectations.

Fortunately, the staff at Kingscott Secondary School were keen to help, and with the support of a teaching assistant, Lara's first few weeks went surprisingly well. However, at six minutes past ten on a Tuesday morning, Lara was totally immersed in her history textbook reading about the Gunpowder Plot when her world shattered. The fire alarm on the wall above her desk shrieked. The noise shot through her body with a bolt of physical pain. The pupils leapt from their seats, and she was swept out of the classroom and into the massive glass-domed hall that was the hub of the school. Alarm bells rang discordantly from every corridor, and hundreds of pupils poured from their classrooms, creating a seething mass of humanity, flowing around the balcony and down the stairs towards the exits. Lara felt blinded by the noise, unable to think or breathe. People pressed around her. She couldn't see; every nerve in her brain was dazzled. She found herself pushed up against the cool glass of the balcony and slid down on to the floor, curling into a ball like a hedgehog, desperately trying to defend herself from the onslaught of the world. Feet trampled past her; people called her name, hands reached for her, trying to encourage her to stand. Desperately, she clung to the post of the balcony and she screamed – she screamed like a wounded animal.

Her desperate expression of terror was so loud that she began to focus on the sound of her own voice and the deep breath she took before each cry. She didn't notice the forest of legs start to thin and fade away as the pupils made their way outside. She was unaware of the two adults sitting near to her on the floor, whispering calm words, nor did she sense their relief when the alarm bells stopped and Lara's cries became the only noise echoing around the massive empty hall. She had no idea of time, just the perception that her screams and the rocking motion of her body were the only sensations in her world.

More than a thousand pupils and teachers waited quietly outside as their names were checked off on the class registers. Confused, wide-eyed glances were exchanged as persistent screams drifted from the open windows of the atrium. Teachers whispered in small groups and eventually the entire school filed back to their classrooms, using two small staircases at the back of the building.

When her mother came to collect her after a call from the deputy headteacher, Lara was numb with shock. She never returned to Kingscott Secondary School.

Lara had recently started at Highfield, her fourth school so far. She remembered her three previous schools in intense visual flashes, as if all her memories and emotions were condensed into a mental photo album of her education. If she flicked through those memories in her mind, the stressful images were the most dominant. There had been good times – memories of Mrs Bingle's class were sunny and peaceful – but her mind also held endless scenes of confusion, filled with faces and words that she did not understand. Lots of her memories were blank pages, plain black when the world had become such a buzz and swirl of turmoil that she had retreated into the darkness of her own mind.

It was almost impossible to think about the short time that she had spent at Kingscott Secondary School. Just recalling the central atrium of the school made her heart thud and her breath come in short, sharp gulps as the panic flooded back. She shuddered, recalling the crush of hundreds of pupils pouring out of classrooms into the hall, their voices echoing off the ceiling and flowing down on to her in a torrent of overwhelming noise that she couldn't escape.

Now, as she walked down the corridor to her new headteacher's office, Lara came back to the question that always bumped around in her mind. Was school the best time of her life? Every day there had been stressful because it was so unfamiliar. Being part of this new school was like swimming in a massive shoal of fish that was dashing to and fro in a frenzy of purpose. She was being swept along with them but with little understanding of where she was going, what she was doing or what potential threats might be lurking around each corner.

Reflecting on her experience so far, she struggled to believe that school would be the best time of her life. For life to be bearable, Lara had to hope that there would be better days to come.

Chapter Three

Mr Harris looked up and smiled when Lara came into the room.

"Ah, Lara . . . what a surprise to see you here," he said jovially. The girl stared up at her new headteacher with her brows knitted in anxious confusion. She knew that being sent to Mr Harris meant that she was in trouble, but she was never quite sure how the trouble began. Also, usually when she had done something wrong, the old people would raise their voices and start wagging their fingers at her. Mr Harris didn't react like that, which made him even more confusing.

"Why are you surprised to see me, Mr Harris?" she ventured. She thought that perhaps he wasn't as able to remember the facts as well as she could, so she attempted to explain the logic of the situation. "I was sent to your office six times last week. So that means that on average I should be sent here four more times before Friday."

Mr Harris looked across at Lara fondly, noting her earnest, nervous manner and sighed. "Yes, Lara, I totally agree. It was silly of me to say it was surprising. Come in and we can have a chat." He smiled at Lara and led the way into his office. "Janice, could we have two cups of tea, please," he asked his secretary as he passed her desk.

"Yes, Mr Harris," answered Janice. "Is that black with one sugar in the yellow cup, Lara?"

   DOI: 10.4324/9781003208044-4

Lara looked at her, puzzled for a moment. "I always have it that way," she replied before following Mr Harris through the door.

Janice laughed to herself as she rose to put on the kettle. She was quite a small lady who usually wore home-made woolly cardigans hiding her waist, which was not as slender as it had been in her younger years. Janice had a habit of knitting while watching nail-biting murder mysteries on television. Her cardigans often ended up an unusual shape, perhaps with one sleeve longer than the other, if she had been distracted by a particularly daring police rescue at a critical moment in the garment's design. Despite her hairy cardigans, Janice was adored by the staff and pupils of Highfield Secondary School. She was a welcoming, maternal character who knew everything – she knew when a pupil was grieving for a grandparent, she knew how to clear paper jams from the depths of the printer and she always knew how to ask the right question when someone was in distress. Janice solved problems. She had a smile for anyone who entered her office and a comfortable shoulder for those who just needed to have a good cry.

She stood waiting for the kettle to boil and glanced down at her shoes. The left one was elegant and perfectly formed. The right one looked as though it had been run over by a lawnmower. Janice stared woefully at her chewed shoe and resolved that this was the last time she was going to own a puppy.

Marcus Harris moved to sit behind his desk. He was a small man with sandy-coloured hair and bushy eyebrows that wriggled when he talked. His eyes almost disappeared when he laughed, leaving a fine web of contented wrinkles around them when his face relaxed. He loved life and laughed easily, often letting out great chuckles that seemed unbecoming of a headteacher. But his laughter was infectious, and his good humour tended to spread through the school, as teachers and students alike could not help smiling in his wake. His desk was piled with neat stacks of books and paperwork, and he spent long hours in his office ensuring that the school ran smoothly. He peered over his in-tray at Lara who was standing uncomfortably by the door, following the usual routine of being reluctant to sit down. Normally, he let her linger by the door, but today he wanted her to sit and relax while they talked.

"Sit down, Lara," he said, indicating the sofa.

Lara looked accusingly at the sofa, which was the only available seat in the office, and then perched gingerly on the very edge as if she had been asked to sit on a dead animal. Janice arrived with the tea, and Lara cupped it in her hands, apparently finding reassurance from its warmth. Mr Harris swiftly checked his emails and found a summary of Lara's latest offence from her Maths teacher, Miss Fisher:

Dear Mr Harris,

Normally, Lara Frost is shy and withdrawn in my lessons, but today she has been quite impossible and terribly rude. I asked her to sit in a different seat from usual so that she could meet some different pupils, and she flatly refused, saying that she always sat next to the wall. She spent much of the lesson with her hands over her ears and then told me that my bottom was three sizes larger than the national average. I'm sorry, but I have sent her to you because she has completely destroyed my authority in this lesson.

Best wishes,
Louisa
Miss Louisa Fisher
Maths Teacher, Highfield Secondary School

Mr Harris's mouth twitched with amusement, and he took a slug of tea to drown the laughter that was threatening to escape.

"So, Lara, what happened with Miss Fisher?"

Lara frowned. She was finding it hard to remember the names of all the teachers in this new school and wasn't sure to whom Mr Harris was referring. "Is she the old person who teaches me Maths?" she asked innocently.

Old! thought Mr Harris. *If Lara thinks Miss Fisher is old, she must think I'm a dinosaur!*

"She certainly teaches you Maths," he said aloud, "but I think it is unkind to call her old."

"I'm sorry. I'm sorry. All adults are old," replied Lara. Mr Harris decided not to argue the point.

"Did Miss Fisher ask you to sit in a different seat?"

"Yes."

"So why did you not do as she asked?"

"I don't like sitting in different seats. It makes me . . ." Lara searched for a word to describe how her body felt when she had to do something unexpected. "Jumpy," she concluded.

Lara folded her arms and gritted her teeth. The texture of Mr Harris's sofa was really difficult to ignore. She could feel the horrid hairy fronds of the fabric touching the back of her legs. It was dirty and old. Hundreds of people must have sat on it, leaving stray hairs and flakes of redundant skin. She breathed deeply, trying to calm her desire to leap up and start shouting. She knew that it never ended well when she began shouting, but she could feel the pressure building up inside her. She swiftly put the remains of her tea on a side table, crossed her arms and began rocking backwards and forwards on the edge of the sofa. Mr Harris cocked his head to one side, absorbing the discomfort that was radiating from Lara's body language.

"Lara, what's making you so uncomfortable at the moment?"

"The sofa," came the instant reply.

"I know it's old and tatty, but what exactly is upsetting you?"

Mr Harris's eyebrows wriggled into an unaccustomed frown. Normally, he was good at helping pupils to feel at ease when talking to him, and yet Lara Frost looked as tense as a coiled spring. She stood up and sidled over to the window, looking back at the saggy sofa in disgust, trying to translate the sensations that she was experiencing into words. So often her mind became fuzzy and uncontrolled with ideas and images rocketing around, refusing to be ignored. Mr Harris waited while she gathered her thoughts.

"It's the prickling itch on the back of my legs. The different browns look all wrong, and there's a stain on the arm and holes in the seat. That hairy fabric is almost impossible to clean, so it will be full of dirt and germs that will be breeding every second. It makes me feel as though something is pressing on my heart and my breathing starts to go too fast."

Wow, thought Mr Harris, looking at the shabby sofa with new eyes. *I knew it was bad but not that bad.*

"I see," he replied, trying not to sound offended.

"And it's very poorly designed," Lara continued. "If it had been made properly, the springs wouldn't be poking through the fabric."

"I see," repeated Mr Harris. "Clearly, your knowledge of sofa design exceeds my own," he continued, trying to lighten the mood.

"Yes, it does."

"Ah! Of course, I remember now. Your father makes furniture," said Mr Harris. Lara nodded. He got up and went to the outer office, returning with a wooden chair which he placed near Lara by the window. "Would that be better?"

"Yes," she replied and then belatedly added, "thank you." Her mother was always reminding her to say 'thank you'. Often saying 'thank you' did make sense, but she found it hard to understand why she had to say 'thank you' for things she didn't like, such as the pink fluffy socks Granny Edith had given her for Christmas.

Mr Harris tried to remember what they had been discussing before being told that his old sofa was more revolting than he had realised.

"So, Miss Fisher . . . perhaps she wanted you to move seats so you could work with some different pupils, to get to know them?"

Lara frowned. "She didn't say that." The girl thought for a bit. "I'm not very good at talking in class. I do it at the wrong time or in the wrong way."

Mr Harris changed tack. "And why did you put your hands over your ears?"

"Someone was mowing the grass. It was noisy. I concentrate better when there is less noise."

"OK," said Mr Harris, making a note on the pad in front of him. "But, Lara, if you put your hands over your ears in class, it may look as though you are deliberately not listening, which teachers are likely to find rude."

"I didn't need to listen. I had already understood it when she explained it the first time."

Mr Harris paused and took a deep breath. Lara looked out of the window. Her arms were wrapped around her torso and her shoulders were hunched up near her ears.

"Lara, did you mention something to Miss Fisher about her bottom?"

"Yes, I said it was three sizes larger than average."

Mr Harris tried hard not to smile. "Why on earth did you say that?" he retorted, attempting to sound stern.

Lara's answer came out in a rush. "Well, we were doing averages in class and working out the mean age of the class. I wanted to include Miss Fisher's age in the calculation but she wouldn't say how old she was. She just said that she was below average compared with most teachers in school. Well, that might be true for age, but it is clear from looking at her that her bottom is much larger than an average teacher's bottom. So, she's not completely below average."

Mr Harris let out a small chuckle which he rapidly turned into a cough. He thought about poor Miss Fisher. She was a very good teacher and at twenty-six years old she was below the average age for the school staff. She did have an extraordinarily large bottom. Her small waist only made her bottom seem larger by comparison. It seemed to defy gravity and hung behind her like an afterthought. He knew that curvy figures were thought to be attractive, but Miss Fisher really was curvier than most.

Mr Harris checked his watch, noting that it was the end of the lesson.

"Lara, you are a clever girl."

"I know," she responded matter-of-factly.

"You need to learn two things from today," Mr Harris continued. "First, teachers may think you are being rude if you put your hands over your ears while they are talking, and second, it is best not to comment on the size of someone's bottom – ever. Can you remember that?"

"Yes, Mr Harris."

"Now, go back to class, apologise to Miss Fisher and try to keep out of trouble for the rest of the day." Lara stood up and gave the sofa a wide berth as she left the room.

"Goodbye, Lara," Mr Harris called after her, but she did not reply.

By the time Lara had found her way back to Miss Fisher's class, the next lesson had begun. She scanned the room, looking for her books. Miss Fisher pointed to where they had been left on a desk at the back of the class. Twenty-nine pairs of eyes tracked Lara's movement across the room. They noted the way that she fumbled with her books and then returned to stand awkwardly by the door.

Lara knew she ought to follow Mr Harris's instructions and apologise to Miss Fisher, although she didn't fully understand why she had to apologise for telling the truth. Miss Fisher was writing on the board, explaining a complex sum to the Year 9 class. Her buttocks wobbled in time to the movement of her arm as she wrote. Someone sniggered. Miss Fisher paused mid-calculation, noticing Lara lingering by the door.

"Yes, what is it, Lara?" she asked in a slightly irritated manner.

"I'm sorry that I said that your bottom was much larger than average," Lara said in a neutral tone. She waited for the response of *That's all right, Lara* which she usually received when she apologised to an adult for one of her social blunders. Instead, there was an explosion of gasps and laughter from the Year 9 pupils.

Miss Fisher seemed to be frozen in time, poised at the whiteboard, pen in hand and mouth open. She was apparently unable to speak. Very slowly, she put down the whiteboard pen, turned to face the class and lowered the sizeable bottom on to her chair behind the desk. There was a long pause while Lara lurked by the door, waiting for a response. The pupils were totally silent now, glancing between Miss Fisher and the girl by the door. Finally, Miss Fisher spoke.

"Lara, I think you should go to your next lesson; you will be late."

"OK," Lara replied cheerfully, glad to have a clear instruction to follow, and she left the room. As the door closed behind her, she heard squeals of laughter and a rush of chattering. Lara assumed that someone in the class had said something funny.

Chapter Four

After Lara had left his office, Marcus Harris stared out of the window, absorbing the vibrant colours of the summer's day. The beech leaves had just unfurled and looked crisp and almost unnaturally green. The branches stretched to the sky, basking in the May sunshine. He closed his eyes for a second and then called, "Janice, could you set up an appointment for Mr and Mrs Frost to come and see me as soon as possible?"

"Yes, Mr Harris."

The headteacher sat chewing his lip in thought until he was disturbed by the door to the outer office slamming and Janice's voice at a higher pitch than usual.

"It's not a very good time, Mr Prendergast. Mr Harris is teaching in a few minutes."

"I'm sure he'll make time for me," came the familiar nasal whine.

Mr Harris groaned and began summoning his courage as the door flew open and Eric Prendergast, one of the Design and Technology teachers, barged into his office.

"It won't do! I just won't have it!" whinged Mr Prendergast, pacing up and down the office a couple of times before settling himself on the sofa, as if he intended to stay for a considerable time. Mr Harris tried to muster a smile but found that his face was reluctant to cooperate.

"Eric, here we are again," he said as calmly as possible, trying to keep the exasperation out of his voice. "What seems to be the problem this time?"

 DOI: 10.4324/9781003208044-5

"I just won't have it," repeated Mr Prendergast. "The children in this school have no respect. No respect at all."

It is very hard to respect hair that looks like an unwashed poodle, thought Mr Harris, watching Mr Prendergast's mass of blond wavy hair jiggle about as he ranted. The fact that he had an unusually long red nose did not help the situation. But it was Mr Prendergast's temperament that really caused the pupils to mock him – Mr Prender-ghastly was his nickname. Mr Harris had never encountered someone so persistently angry, and he was fed up with Eric Prendergast bursting into his office, showering him with fury and then leaving a cloud of discontent behind him, infecting Mr Harris's thoughts for the rest of the day.

"Has anything specific happened?" enquired Mr Harris. "Or is this just a general complaint?"

"Someone has been in my classroom!" stated Mr Prendergast with an outraged glare.

"It's not uncommon for people to enter classrooms in a school, Eric," sighed Mr Harris, already aware that this complaint was going to be a waste of his time.

"Yes. But it is not usual to meddle with the teacher's sheep!" whined Mr Prendergast, leaning forward on the sofa and jabbing his finger in Mr Harris's direction.

"Sheep?" questioned Mr Harris, beginning to think that the DT teacher had lost his mind. A tiny snigger came from the outer office, where Janice was clearly able to hear the conversation through the open door.

"I have a collection of treasured, hand-crafted sheep, displayed by the window. There is a clear sign next to them saying 'DO NOT TOUCH'." Mr Prendergast paused for dramatic effect. "Someone has touched them!" he announced as if he was declaring a point of tremendous importance, like aliens landing on the playing field during lunchtime.

Mr Harris rubbed his temples, trying not to think about all the essential things he could be doing rather than listening to Eric Prendergast complaining about his wooden sheep. "And you know that they have been touched because they've moved position?" ventured the headteacher. The end of Mr Prendergast's nose began going purple with outrage.

"They have been placed on top of each other to look as though they are making babies!" spluttered Mr Prendergast.

Mr Harris's face began to twitch. "How extraordinary. I thought sheep made lambs, not babies," he replied jovially. Mr Prendergast scowled at him. The headteacher knew he was about to laugh, so he quickly reached for his handkerchief and began pretending to blow his nose.

"And that is not all," continued Mr Prendergast with a flourish. "Three of the sheep have done poos!"

This was too much for Mr Harris. A great bellow of laughter escaped from his mouth, and he could feel tears of mirth threatening to run down his face.

Mr Prendergast had paused and was watching the headteacher's reaction through narrowed eyes when Janice glided into the office. "Chocolate biscuit, Mr Prendergast?" she offered innocently, momentarily distracting him by thrusting a biscuit tin into his face. It gave Mr Harris a precious moment to stifle the chuckles rising in his throat. Janice winked at him as she retreated to her desk in the outer office.

"Presumably, it's not real poo?" clarified Mr Harris.

"No, made of brown plasticine, but it looks very realistic."

"Well, I'm sorry that you have been distressed by this incident, but it sounds like a harmless practical joke to me," said Mr Harris briskly.

"Practical joke?" spat Mr Prendergast. "How can I teach when my sheep look as though they are having sexual intercourse on the window ledge?"

"Well, it might be best to defuse the situation by putting the sheep away for a while. Or perhaps you could join in the joke by carving a couple of lambs to join the flock and engaging in a helpful discussion about reproduction?" suggested Mr Harris.

"I teach DT, not Biology," replied Mr Prendergast, munching through a chocolate biscuit.

"Well, I will certainly take note of your concerns Eric, but I think I will leave the mystery of the frisky sheep in your capable hands. Now, I'm teaching in a couple of minutes, so we will have to draw this discussion to a close."

Mr Prendergast got up and wandered over to the window, placing the last of the biscuit in his mouth. He looked out at the glorious early summer's day; the fresh, neatly clipped grass dappled in a lazy shade by the surrounding beech trees.

"It's not rained for a bit," he said dolefully.

"Indeed, the weather has been fabulous since the beginning of term," agreed Mr Harris in a positive tone.

"There'll probably be a drought by the end of the month," commented Mr Prendergast, managing to leave the familiar whiff of gloom behind him.

Good gracious! He can even make a summer's day sound miserable, thought Mr Harris. He closed his eyes as the DT teacher left his office but then suddenly called after him.

"Eric, wait . . . Can you tell me one **positive** thing that you've noticed while at school in the last week?"

Eric Prendergast turned around, looking genuinely confused. He muttered, "Well . . . I'm not sure what to say . . ."

Mr Harris gave him a bit more time to think, but for once Eric Prendergast was speechless. He slunk away.

"Hmm, I suspected as much," murmured the headteacher, before turning back to his desk.

"Janice, could you come in for a minute?" he called to the outer office. It was a few moments before Janice appeared and she seemed to be crying. "Janice, my dear. Whatever's wrong?" asked Mr Harris in concern.

"I'm sorry, Mr Harris," she laughed, wiping her eyes. "But I couldn't help overhearing about the sheep. I never thought you would receive a complaint about sheep making babies in the DT department!"

Mr Harris giggled. "I wish I knew which pupils had done it," he said. "I'd pat them on the back myself."

When Lara left school at the end of the afternoon, she was utterly exhausted. Highfield Secondary School was smaller and less stressful than Kingscott, but it still took all her willpower and concentration to make it through the endless interactions, instructions, mysteries, sensations, confusions, terrors, hustle, bustle and banter of a typical school afternoon. It was such a relief to be alone. She could be herself, rather than always trying to be normal.

She put on her headphones as she left the school gate and began the twenty-minute walk through the streets to her home. She liked focusing on the rhythmic thumping of her feet as she marched along, frequently breaking her stride to ensure that she did not tread on any lines in the pavement.

Over time, Lara had learnt to tolerate other people walking on lines. Her mother had written a Social Story™ about lines, which explained that it was safe to walk on them. But when Lara was alone, walking home from school, she found her routine of sticking to the squares comforting. It was safe and predictable, and her mind liked to think of nothing but the movement of her feet and the patterns of the lines and squares as she made her way home.

She pushed open the green front door, dropped her bag at the foot of the stairs and headed to the kitchen. She buttered her toast and smeared it with marmalade, while waiting for the kettle to boil, and then took a cup of black tea with one sugar and the two slices of toast into the Quiet Room, a small sitting room at the back of the house. Pickle, the family dog, trotted in from the garden, delighted to see her return. She bent down and stroked his ears affectionately. Her dad was probably in his workshop but she didn't want to join him today. She needed to be alone with James Bond for a bit.

Lara adored James Bond films. She watched them again and again and again. There was something reassuring about the music and the way that the bad guys always looked bad. But what Lara loved most were the gadgets. She adored the fancy cars, rocket packs, deadly bowler hats and, of course, best of all, the man-eating sofa. Lara settled herself in an armchair, and Pickle curled himself into a warm furry ball on her lap. She searched for *The Living Daylights* and then fast-forwarded to her favourite scene. There was Q showing Mr Bond all the best gadgets that he could use on his latest mission. And there it was – the sofa. Lara's eyes were glued to the screen while the research assistant sat on the sofa and then swiftly disappeared as the seat and sofa back rotated and settled again, leaving no clue that a person was underneath. She rewound and replayed, rewound and replayed, each time fascinated by the way the seat glided round and settled smoothly back into place. This intriguing piece of furniture had been the inspiration for her latest project, which was now almost complete. Lara's whole brain was focused on the screen and the wonders of the man-eating sofa, so she was too slow to react when shrieking voices filled the hall. Pickle scuttled behind the armchair, and a second later the door flew open and three small children galloped into the room.

"Lara! Lara! Lara!" cried her twin cousins, cantering round in circles pretending to be horses.

"My pony's called Snowy," shouted her sister Amelia, cantering her imaginary horse around the room in figures of eight. Either Amelia had been secretly drinking Mr Frost's beer or Snowy was a very naughty imaginary pony because Amelia lurched around the room crashing into the furniture, bouncing off her cousins and knocking the remains of Lara's toast on to the floor. Lara stared at her toast in dismay, trying to process the sudden intrusion.

"Hi, Lara." Her brother, Teddy, appeared round the door and then disappeared again. Lara blinked. She needed to stop the film and reached for the remote control, but one of the twins galloped into her arm knocking the control to the floor. The back flew off and the batteries rolled away under the chair.

"Come and play with us," squawked the twins, galloping all over the remote control and mashing her toast into the carpet with their small, persistent feet.

"You can be the mummy horse. Snowy loves his mummy," yelled Amelia, throwing her arms around Lara's legs and making strange, high whinnying sounds.

Lara seemed to be holding her breath; she felt dizzy and disorientated. A rushing noise filled her ears and a stiff band seemed to be tightening around her chest. James Bond was still moving across the screen, but she couldn't see him because the twins were blocking her view. She tried to stand but Amelia was clinging to her legs. She needed to run.

"Get off, Amelia," she shouted. Her panic was rising as she tried to run again, but her legs were caught in a web of little arms. It seemed impossible that four-years-olds could be so strong. "Get off!" she screamed again, fighting to free her legs.

Amelia's grip slackened for a moment, and Lara kicked out with her right leg, flinging her sister's small body across the room to land with a dull thud against the wall. Lara fled. She didn't see her mother lumbering through the front door, laden with bags of groceries. She didn't notice her brother in the kitchen, as he swiftly flattened himself against the cooker to give her room to pass. She was like a bolting carthorse wearing blinkers. Oblivious to anything on either side, she charged through the back door, across the lawn and up the steps of the treehouse. At the top, she slammed the door and locked it behind her and then collapsed to lie panting on the warm wooden floor.

"I'm sorry. I'm sorry. I'm sorry . . . I'm sorry. I'm sorry. I'm sorry," she said over and over again to herself. Lara had learnt quite soon after starting school that saying sorry was usually the right thing to do when something went wrong, even though she often did not understand why she was apologising. The phrase had become a comforting mantra she chanted to herself when trying to calm down.

A moment later, Pickle pushed his way through a small dog-sized hole in the planking. He lay down beside Lara with his head on her shoulder. She turned on her side and wrapped herself around his warm, fuzzy body, feeling her breathing adjust to match his calm contented slumber.

In the kitchen, Mrs Frost dried Amelia's tears and suggested that the imaginary horses grazed in the garden while the children had some tea. Teddy and Mrs Frost unpacked the shopping. Amelia and the twins sat at the kitchen table eating slices of toast and apples. Mrs Frost rounded up the batteries from under the chairs and scraped the worst of the marmalade and crumbs off the carpet.

Lara had no idea how long she lay in the treehouse. Time for her had always been a strange elastic concept that was prone to speeding up or slowing down, depending on her mood or situation. She lay listening to the birds, the distant hum of traffic from the main road and the rhythmical rasping of her father cutting wood in the workshop.

Then she heard her mother's voice from below.

"Lara. I'm coming up. Open the door. I'm bringing tea." Lara sat up and unbolted the treehouse door, while Mrs Frost carefully negotiated the ramp with a mug of hot tea in each hand.

"Hello," she said simply, handing over the tea to Lara.

"I'm sorry. I'm sorry. I'm sorry," Lara said automatically. They sat side by side in the treehouse, clasping the mugs with Pickle nestled on Lara's lap.

"I'm sorry, too," replied her mother. "They burst into the house while I was getting the shopping out of the car."

Lara slurped her tea. "I know you find it hard if people surprise you when you're relaxing," Mrs Frost continued. Lara nodded. "You'll have to apologise to Amelia. You know you shouldn't hurt other people, even when you are feeling cross."

"I know." They sipped their tea in silence for a minute.

"Just think," said Mrs Frost, "in a few days, you'll have finished the sofa and you won't be tormented by the little ones each night."

Lara smiled. "It's going to be perfect," she said. "Can I use it for Great Aunt Mabel as well?"

"Hmm. We'll have to set some rules. You can't just use it to avoid meeting everyone who comes to the house. Let's get it working first and then we can plan how it should be used."

Chapter Five

The following day did not go well for Lara. She forgot her packed lunch and so felt jittery all morning, dreading the challenge of navigating the dining hall at lunchtime. She was slow to pack up her books before lunch and ambled reluctantly towards the school hall. She hated lunchtimes; they were so noisy and baffling. It was only her second week at Highfield Secondary School. In the first week, she had brought a packed lunch and on three days had managed to eat it in a quiet corner of the Year 7 cloakrooms. But on two days a teacher had insisted that she ate in the dining room.

There were so many problems with the dining hall – the sheer number of people for a start and then there was the question of where to sit. She knew people thought it was odd if she sat by herself, and yet something always seemed to go wrong if she sat with other people. Nervously she joined the queue, not sure what she ought to be doing. She shuffled down the line, clutching a tray, uncertain how to respond when the old people behind the counter asked her questions. She ended up with some kind of minced slop on her plate.

"What is it?" she asked the rosy-cheeked woman with a hairnet who had dumped it on her tray.

"Lasagne," replied the old person. Lara stared at her plate. The mush couldn't be lasagne. It didn't look anything like the lasagne her mother cooked. The pasta was green and the mince looked as though there were chopped carrots in

   DOI: 10.4324/9781003208044-6

it, which wasn't right. She was about to ask again, but the dinner lady had moved on and was attending to children behind Lara. She was pushed to the end of the counter where she found a reassuringly recognisable apple and a banana, which she added to her tray. She turned to face the tables to find that almost every seat was taken. She could feel her hand starting to shake, which often happened when she was unsettled. The noise in the hall and the lasagne issues were starting to stress her out. She needed to sit down quickly before she dropped her tray. She headed for the nearest empty seat and sat down. After staring at the slop on her plate, Lara finally decided it looked too dangerous to eat and so began peeling the banana. In an effort to relax, she tuned out of the noise of the hall and concentrated on chewing each piece of banana ten times.

Suddenly, she felt a sharp pain and she realised that the girl next to her was knocking on her forehead as if she was a door.

"Hey, bonehead, I was talking to you. Are you deaf as well as weird?" Lara turned to her left, to see a pair of intense blue eyes scowling at her. Being new to the school, she had not yet encountered Julia Smythe. Julia was a couple of years older, with a mature, curvy figure. She glided around the school with a herd of glossy-haired, empty-headed admirers, who spent most of their free time pouting at their phones. There was usually never a free space at Julia's table, but one of the admirers had just left to meet her boyfriend. Lara had unfortunately taken the empty seat, unaware that no one **ever** sat next to Julia Smythe without being invited. Even worse, Julia was in Miss Fisher's Year

9 Maths set and had witnessed the 'large bottom apology' the day before.

Julia had long golden hair due to regular visits to the hairdresser and lots of bottles of hair dye. Her large eyes and long fluttery eyelashes would have given her an angelic look, were it not for the thickly applied mascara, her twisted expression and the spiteful words pouring out of her mouth. She knocked again on Lara's head, rubbing her knuckles into the younger girl's forehead. The unexpected physical contact flooded Lara with feelings of alarm.

"I'm sorry. I'm sorry. I'm sorry," she mumbled to herself.

"I said, are you deaf as well as weird?" Julia looked around the table, gathering support for Lara's humiliation from among her peers. Lara had no idea how to reply so she said nothing.

"You dumb? Has the cat got your tongue? Idiot!" sneered Julia, shaking her curls very prettily for the benefit of the boys carrying their trays past her line of sight. The other girls tittered admiringly as if Julia had just said something clever and funny. "Maybe you told all your friends that they had 'larger than average bottoms' like Miss Fisher and so nobody wants to sit with poor Lara the weirdo."

Lara couldn't cope with the rush of words and was still trying to process the first sentence. She replied, "I haven't seen any cats and I am not an idiot. That's an old-fashioned word that indicates that someone has a profound mental disability. I'm quite clever, so it's not appropriate to call me an idiot."

Julia was momentarily silenced. This was not the response she had been expecting. She had assumed that

Lara would just move to another table. After a brief pause, she recovered, turning the situation back to her advantage. "No, you're right, you're not an idiot; you're something even worse – a geek. We don't sit with geeks, you might infect us with geekitis." This comment made the other girls laugh again, and Julia smirked, soaking up her friends' admiration. Lara sat awkwardly, her half-chewed banana still in her hand.

Julia suddenly jumped to her feet and yelled, "Can't you take a hint! You're a weird geek! Move!" and then she hissed, "Never try to sit with me again . . . Never!" The conversation in the dining room had stilled and nearly five hundred pupils stared at Lara as she got up from the table, clutching her lunch tray in both hands.

"I'm sorry. I'm sorry. I'm sorry," she said automatically. She was not sure what to do; all the seats on the tables near her were taken. She could feel her hands shaking violently and hear a rushing noise in her ears, which she recognised as a sign of panic. She had to leave. She dumped her lunch tray back on the table next to Julia and bolted for the exit.

Julia yelled after her. "Oi, nerd! Clear up your own lunch. It's not my job."

"Actually, Julia, it has just become your job," stated a cool voice behind her. Julia groaned noisily and looked up to see Mr Thornhill, Head of Design and Technology, glowering down at her.

"You should all clear this table and leave now," said Mr Thornhill.

"But I haven't eaten my pudding yet," interrupted Julia's neighbour sulkily.

"I said **now**," repeated Mr Thornhill very quietly, but each pupil at the table felt the menace in his voice. Five of the girls swiftly rose and returned their trays to the dirty tray stand. Julia glowered at Mr Thornhill. She stood up, painfully slowly, and slouched over to put away her tray. The dining room remained in silence as the whole school watched the scene play out. Julia joined her friends and led the way to the exit, flicking her hair over her shoulder and rolling her eyes in disgust.

Clearly but quietly, Mr Thornhill's voice carried across the room. "Julia, you seem to have forgotten to clear the last tray on your table," he said, pointing to Lara's tray.

"It's not my tray and I am not your slave, Sir. I don't tidy up after other people," retorted Julia, turning again to the exit.

"Julia Smythe, I am not asking you to be a slave but I am expecting you to clear up the mess that **you** created by humiliating a pupil who is not only younger than you but also new to this school. Remove that tray now or the consequences for you will be worse than you can imagine." The hall held its breath. Julia's friends edged away from her as they did not want to be polluted by her disgrace. After a long pause, Julia sauntered over to the table and collected the tray. Mr Thornhill removed the apple from it as she passed. She held the tray high on one hand like an elegant French waitress before crashing it down on the dirty tray stand, making the cutlery on the other trays jump and clatter. Alone, she stalked out of the hall.

The pupils who were still eating lunch took a collective intake of breath.

Mr Thornhill tossed the apple high in the air and caught it with a flourish. He wandered to the back of the hall and waited until the buzz of conversation resumed. Then he approached a small boy with blond hair and a smattering of freckles across his nose who was sitting on the edge of a boisterous group of Year 7 children, watching the conversation, but not contributing to it.

Mr Thornhill squatted down beside him, "Hello, Dylan." Dylan blinked at the teacher warily. Mr Thornhill continued, "Lara forgot her apple when she left the hall. Would you mind taking it to her, please?"

Dylan looked at him with big serious eyes for a moment and then nodded. "Where is she?"

"Well, that's the tricky bit; I'm not sure where she will have gone. But I am guessing it will be a quiet place outside. Would you mind having a look?"

"OK," he replied.

"One last thing Dylan – when you find her, please stay with her until she has finished the apple." Dylan looked puzzled by this request but nodded again in agreement.

Mr Thornhill watched Dylan tuck the apple into his pocket and leave the hall. Then he slipped out into the corridor and strode towards the headteacher's office, humming under his breath as he went.

"Afternoon, Janice. How's that puppy of yours?" he asked as he entered the outer office. Janice grimaced and stuck her foot out from under the desk to show the chewed toe of her favourite shoes.

"He's gorgeous and maddening at the same time," she replied.

"Ha! I suspect that my wife might describe me like that," Mr Thornhill laughed, "although at least I don't chew her shoes."

Janice giggled. "Oh, Mr Thornhill – you do make me laugh! Mr Harris is in his office if you need a word."

Robert Thornhill knocked briefly and then popped his head round the door to the headteacher's office.

Mr Harris looked up from his desk and greeted him warmly. "Hello, Robert. How nice to see you. Come in, come in. What brings you to my lair?"

"I won't keep you long," Mr Thornhill assured him, perching on the arm of the saggy sofa, "but I'm worried about the new girl who's just joined Year 7."

"Lara Frost?"

"Yes. That's the one."

"Funny you should mention her just now," replied Mr Harris. "I've asked her parents to meet me this afternoon. What are your concerns?"

"I suppose my main worry is that she doesn't seem very happy, but I think it's more than that. I know that joining a new school in the middle of Year 7 is difficult, but she reacts differently compared with her peers and doesn't pick up on the social cues that most young people would instinctively understand."

"I completely agree and several other teachers have made similar observations. Mr Prendergast said she was difficult when he told her off last week for being late for lessons."

"Eric Prendergast finds all young people difficult," interrupted Mr Thornhill. "It was Lara's first week at Highfield last week. The poor girl was probably lost. I'm sorry, Marcus, but Eric Prendergast is completely unsuited to being a teacher."

"Yes, I'm afraid I agree with you. Finding a way to encourage Eric to move on to a different career is another one of my problems, but not one I can solve today." The longer hairs in Mr Harris's eyebrows waggled as he frowned. "I've talked with Lara several times, and I feel she has significant difficulties with social interaction and sensory processing. I wouldn't be surprised if she was on the autism spectrum and yet her parents have not mentioned any difficulties."

"What school did she come from?"

Mr Harris brought up Lara's school record on his computer screen.

"She started at Kingscott in September, but she didn't settle there, and I think she's been educated at home for the last two terms. The application for her to move here came just before Easter and I've not had any transfer information from Kingscott yet."

"It would be really interesting to hear what they have to say," replied Mr Thornhill.

"Yes, I'll call them this afternoon once I've spoken to her parents," said Mr Harris. "Poor Lara, I suspect that school has been quite tough for her."

"Yes, young people are not always very kind," said Mr Thornhill thoughtfully. "She had a close encounter with Julia Smythe during lunchtime."

"Crikey! I bet that didn't go well. Even I find Julia Smythe terrifying and I'm the headteacher," chuckled Mr Harris.

"Yes. There is something menacing about all the mascara," laughed Mr Thornhill. "Better go. I'm teaching Year 10 in a minute. Let me know how your chat with the Frosts goes."

"I will. Oh, and Robert, are you still up for cycling round Longdown on Sunday?" Mr Thornhill was already halfway out the door.

"Yup, I'll be there," he replied. "Look after your shoes, Janice," he called to Janice's bottom, which was sticking out of the stationery cupboard.

"Bye, Mr Thornhill," answered Janice, who was wrestling a long-armed stapler out of the back of the cupboard. She straightened up and smiled, thinking how lucky she was to have such friendly colleagues. Then she scowled as she spotted her tragically mauled right shoe. If only her puppy was more adorable and less maddening.

After leaving the dining hall, Dylan headed out of the double doors into the school grounds. He knew Lara, as he was in some of the same classes as her, but, like him, she tended to keep herself to herself. He wandered out through the beech trees and looked around the back of the sheds where the sports equipment was stored. He ventured across the sports pitch to the line of trees near the boundary fence. This was where he often liked to sit when he wanted to be alone; with his back up against a tree trunk, he would watch the birds in the hedgerow. However, Lara was not here. He wandered back towards the school buildings and saw pupils starting to emerge into the sunlight for some fresh air after lunch. Looking to the right of the school, his eye was caught by the flash of a line of old DVDs hanging in the sun, scaring the birds off the seedlings in the school vegetable garden. He wandered over, curious to see if the carrots he had helped to plant had come up yet. As he reached the fence, he saw a pair of legs on the grassy path that ran between two beds of vegetables. He paused and then opened the gate and approached the legs.

Lara was sitting with her back against the fence of the vegetable garden, her legs stretched out before her. She looked up at him with wide hazel eyes. Her face looked flushed as if she had been running recently, or possibly crying. Dylan approached cautiously. Lara watched him but did not offer a greeting. Dylan was not sure what to say – he was never very good at starting conversations. After hesitating for a moment, he held out the apple.

"Mr Thornhill said I should bring you this."

Lara took the apple gratefully. "Thank you," she said but did not immediately start eating it. Dylan felt uncomfortable just standing in front of her. However, he had agreed to stay until she had finished the apple, so he sat down beside her and waited.

"Why are you sitting with me?" asked Lara.

"Mr Thornhill said I should stay until you had eaten the apple."

"Oh." Lara looked at the apple and began to eat. She slowly took bite after bite, savouring the crunch and juiciness of the fruit. The boy and girl sat in silence, enjoying the sun on their faces and that, for once, there didn't seem to be a need to talk. After a while, Lara held up the apple core, not sure where to put it as she couldn't see a bin. Dylan stared at it for a bit and then glanced over at a bare patch of earth in the corner of the vegetable garden.

"Let's plant it," he suggested.

Lara shrugged. "Are we allowed to?"

"I don't think it will be a problem. I sometimes help Mrs Bloxham who runs the gardening clubs. I'm sure she won't mind if we plant an apple tree."

"All right." Lara shrugged again. Dylan went to the tool shed and returned with a trowel and a label on a stick. He started digging while Lara wrote 'Lunch apple' on the stick. It didn't take long to drop the apple core into the hole, cover it with soil, water it and press the label into the ground next to it. Dylan rocked back on his heels and grinned at Lara. She smiled back.

"What happens if all the seeds in the core geminate and grow?" she asked.

"I guess we'll pull up some of the seedlings and either plant them somewhere else or put them on the compost heap," Dylan replied.

"What's your name?" Lara asked.

"Dylan. We're in the same Maths set."

"Oh. I'm Lara."

"I know."

"Oh." Then, after a pause, "Dylan, what does 'Has the cat got your tongue?' mean?"

"I'm not sure where the phrase comes from but it's a way of asking why someone doesn't speak. If a cat had taken your tongue, you wouldn't be able to talk."

"So people say it when there aren't any cats around?"

Dylan smiled, "Yes, it is just a figure of speech – you know, like when someone says 'I'm starving', they actually mean 'I'm really hungry'. They don't literally mean what they say."

"Oh," replied Lara. "I wish people did mean what they say. It would make life so much easier."

"Come on, we'll be late for Science," said Dylan, dusting the earth from his knees. "We should sing to the apple tree;

apparently, plants like that," he suggested as they headed back across the sports pitch together.

"It's not a tree yet," commented Lara.

"I know, but maybe it will become one, with some encouragement," laughed Dylan. "Shall we meet here again tomorrow to see how it's getting on?"

"Yeah. All right."

Chapter Six

"Mr and Mrs Frost are here to see you, Mr Harris," called Janice.

"Excellent," replied the headteacher. "Show them in and could you rustle up some tea, please."

Mr Harris rose to meet Lara's parents as they entered his office. He greeted them with a beaming smile and a friendly handshake. He noted that Mrs Frost's handkerchief had been twisted into a bedraggled coil, in an attempt to calm her nerves.

"How nice to see you both again," Mr Harris began. "Please do sit down." He indicated the sofa with his hand.

Mr Frost gazed at the drooping sofa, taking in the shabby brown covers which were made from a hairy material. In places, the fury fabric had been rubbed bald by the countless bottoms that had sat on it over the years. There was a large brown stain on one arm, and in three places the cover had ripped to show an unpleasant grey foam beneath. Mr Frost sat reluctantly. Mrs Frost sat beside her husband and burst into tears.

"Oh dear, I'm terribly sorry, Mrs Frost. The sofa does seem to have an unfortunate effect on many people," spluttered Mr Harris, handing her a box of tissues and pulling up the wooden chair by the window to sit opposite them. Mrs Frost looked bewildered and then focused on the sofa for the first time.

"I wasn't crying about the sofa," she sniffed, "but now you mention it, it does look rather tired."

DOI: 10.4324/9781003208044-7

"It's hideous," admitted Mr Harris. "It was in the staff room for years." He pointed to the brown stain on the arm. "Mr Thornhill's coffee three years ago, and that," pointing to the large rip on the left-hand side, "was caused by Mrs Bloxham's high heels when she climbed on it to water the spider plant." He smiled tenderly at the disgusting piece of furniture. "I fully intend to replace it, but it does bring back fond memories, and there always seems to be more important ways to spend the money."

Mr and Mrs Frost nodded sympathetically.

"Now, I think we should talk about Lara," said the headteacher, and Mrs Frost let out a loud sob. He paused while Janice came in with the tea tray and he passed a mug to Mrs Frost. He glanced out of the window, to allow her a few moments to collect herself, and was surprised to see a small dog sitting purposefully on the grass. It was staring at the main school entrance and was clearly waiting for something to happen. He raised a puzzled eyebrow and drew his attention back to the room, smiling at Lara's parents.

"I think Lara is an absolute cracker. She is honest, hardworking and has a talent for Maths and Science. She has an interesting mind, and I am sure that when she finds her niche, she will be very successful in the adult world." Lara's parents gaped at him over their mugs of tea and said nothing. So Mr Harris pressed on.

"In the short time that Lara has been here, I feel she has demonstrated good potential, but, as you know, she is often involved in social misunderstandings, and I am worried that she is not happy at school." Mr Frost nodded, and Mrs Frost reached for another tissue. "I asked you to come in today so that we could talk through how we can work together to improve Lara's experience of school." Mr Harris paused again, this time waiting for a response.

After a while, Mr Frost swallowed. "I'm sorry, Mr Harris, this is all just a bit of a shock."

"Were you not aware that Lara was unhappy at school?" asked the headteacher.

"Oh no, we knew about that," replied Mr Frost. "It's just . . ." He hesitated and looked down at his feet. "Well, usually when headteachers ask to see us, they don't highlight the good things about Lara in the way you have. Normally, we get told about all the problems she's causing."

A large tear rolled down Mrs Frost's cheek. "I thought you were going to ask Lara to leave the school," she whispered.

"Certainly not," replied Mr Harris. "What on earth gave you that impression?"

"Well, it has happened before," mumbled Mrs Frost.

"Right, let's get one thing straight," said Mr Harris decisively. "Lara is not going to be asked to leave this school, and by the end of the day, we are going to have a plan of action to help her to be happier here." He leaned over to his desk and grasped a pad of paper. "Janice!" he called. "Chocolate biscuits, please! We need food for thought." He smiled warmly at Mr and Mrs Frost, which unfortunately made Mrs Frost burst into a fresh round of sobs, but her husband grinned and rubbed her shoulder.

As the minutes passed, Lara's story gradually emerged, and Mr Harris absorbed the details as the narrative ebbed and flowed around him. Emotions oozed from every sentence, as the tale conveyed the love, confusion, grief, frustration, pride, fear and hope that Lara's family had endured.

The journey had begun when Lara was a toddler and it became clear that she was going to take a different path compared with other children of her age. Her parents knew that the world was an intense and frightening experience for her – full of crowded places, rough textures and bright lights. It seemed impossible for her to communicate her thoughts and feelings, which led to screaming bouts of frustrated rage. Other people were bewildering for her, so it was often easier for Lara to be on her own.

Lara's parents knew that being different could be brutal at school when most children wanted to be the same, just wanting to fit in. In the early days, Lara was an easy target for bullies. There were always some children who liked to make themselves look good by picking on the girl who behaved differently and couldn't think of a witty response to their taunts. Lara pretended that she didn't mind being teased. Often she wasn't even sure what the bullies were teasing her about, but it still hurt. She wanted to have friends

– she just didn't know how to make them. Distress was Lara's constant companion at her first school, and after an unfortunate incident at the local museum, the school staff had suggested very firmly that Lara might be better suited to a different school.

Then there were the people who tried to help. Mrs Frost could list the streams of professionals who had come and gone – speech and language therapists, teachers, occupational therapists, psychologists and doctors. To Lara, these people were just part of life's confusion. They asked lots of questions, scribbled information in notebooks and then often disappeared from her life as quickly as they had arrived. Finally, it was agreed that Lara was autistic and she was given a diagnosis of autism spectrum disorder. The diagnosis arrived like an uninvited guest and made itself at home in the Frost family, with no intention of leaving again. It lurked around their lives like a disgruntled cloud, ready to billow up into a tempestuous storm, or at other times to disperse, leaving periods of clarity and peace.

Lara's parents found her diagnosis helpful as it allowed them to understand her better, and life at home became easier. Lara still found people hard to interpret, but she gradually learnt the rules for interacting with others – the give and take of conversations and that not everyone was as fascinated with James Bond as she was. She steadily learnt to tolerate the unexpected and to listen to the signals that her body sent when she began to feel distressed. As she began to understand how slow, deep breathing and gentle rocking helped her body to calm, her episodes of distress became less frequent.

However, there were times when she was rapidly seized by panic. A sudden crush of people on a train station platform could cause her to be submerged in a swirling fog of chaos, bringing a mess of sensations and feelings. At such times, onlookers often didn't recognise Lara's fear and anxiety. They just saw a girl behaving strangely or being stubborn for no reason. Some caught Mrs Frost's eye with nods of sympathy. A few would ask if they could help. Many tutted to themselves, smugly thinking how **they** would never allow a child to behave so badly in public. They were content in their ignorance of her situation.

Mrs Frost explained the move to Mrs Bingle's class after the incident in the museum and how Lara had made huge progress in the two years she spent in Mrs Bingle's care. Like a parched landscape coming to life after a fall of rain, Lara's mind began to be free to absorb information as her anxiety receded. Mr Frost briefly outlined how Lara's short time at Kingscott Secondary School came to an abrupt end on the day of the fire practice. His wife described how she had heard Lara's exhausted, rasping shrieks down the phone when the deputy headteacher called her.

Lara had been too scared to go to school the following day. When Mr and Mrs Frost met with the headteacher, it was gently suggested that Kingscott was not an appropriate school for her. To the Frosts, this felt as if a door was being slammed in Lara's face, just as she had tried to cross the threshold into secondary education. However, the headteacher's comments were of no consequence. Her parents could see that Lara's mind now associated Kingscott Secondary School with feelings of such terror that any talk of returning there caused her to retreat to the treehouse where she lay on the floor waiting for her trembling to subside.

Mrs Frost had to stop talking at this point in the story to swallow back more tears.

"Poor Lara," murmured Mr Harris. "She must have been terrified."

"Yes," Mr Frost replied. "I think it was really traumatic for her. She has studied at home since then and worked on a project in my workshop. It's been going well, but we felt that she needed to be in school because she has to learn to tolerate the real world."

"We hoped that she might cope better here as the school is only half the size of Kingscott," said Mrs Frost quietly.

"Why didn't you tell me all this when you came to look round the school?" asked Mr Harris. The Frosts glanced at each other.

"I'm sorry, Mr Harris," confessed Mr Frost, "but we thought you might not take her if you knew she had been asked to leave two schools already. We've worked really hard to help her to manage in busy places and to cope with anxiety. We decided it might be better if she didn't arrive with a huge file of reports that highlight all her problems from the past and all the things she can't do."

"I see," said Mr Harris, resting his chin on his hands. "That perhaps wasn't the wisest decision, but I can understand why you thought it was best." He drew in a deep breath, "If I had known about her difficulties, I would have made sure that support was in place for her before she arrived. But never mind. We'll just have to act quickly to ensure that her time here is a positive experience for her." Lara's parents nodded. "I think we should make a list of her strengths and areas of difficulty and brainstorm some ideas of how we can support her. We had better start with a plan to help her cope when a fire alarm goes off."

Forty minutes later, Mr Harris drew the meeting to a close. "I will explain the situation to all Lara's teachers at our staff meeting tomorrow. We have several pupils with similar difficulties to Lara, so we run various activities aimed at helping young people with their social skills. I'll suggest that Lara is included in some of the sessions."

"Thank you so much, Mr Harris," said Mrs Frost.

"Oh, and may I ask if you are in touch with other families who have a child with autism?"

"Well – not really. There was one family we knew, but they moved away," replied Mrs Frost, looking out of the window. She was distracted for a moment when she saw Pickle sitting patiently on the grass outside, waiting for them to re-emerge from the building. He must have followed them all the way to school. She gathered herself again. "If I'm honest, Mr Harris, things were often difficult with other parents at school because of Lara's behaviour, so we learnt to keep ourselves to ourselves."

"Well, I can immediately think of two families who I'm sure would be pleased to meet with you. I suspect they will have faced many of the same challenges that you have, but their children are very well settled here now. One of the mothers is involved in a local autism support group. Would you like me to put you in touch?"

Mrs Frost began blinking and sniffing again.

"That would be very kind, Mr Harris," her husband said quickly.

"Good, good. Now if you will excuse me, I need to teach Year 8 in five minutes, so I had better get a move on. Thank you so much for coming in, Mr and Mrs Frost. Your suggestions have been really helpful."

Mrs Frost heaved herself off the saggy sofa. She clasped Mr Harris's hand in both of hers. "I'm so relieved, Mr Harris, I could kiss you," she said. "Thank you, from the bottom of my heart for helping Lara. She means the world to us."

Mr Harris went rather pink. His bushy eyebrows wriggled in surprise, and he beamed. "My pleasure," he replied.

Mr Frost came forward and gave him a firm handshake.

"You'll excuse me if I don't offer to kiss you, Mr Harris. That's not my style."

"Quite so, quite so," replied the headteacher, smiling.

The Frosts chatted as they retreated down the corridor.

"He's wonderful! He's like Mrs Bingle," exclaimed Mrs Frost.

"Except he's got short hair and doesn't wear a dress," laughed her husband.

"I didn't mean he looks like her, you muppet," Mrs Frost countered, thumping her husband playfully on the arm. "I mean that he instinctively understands Lara and sees her strengths."

"Yes, we've struck gold with him," replied Mr Frost "Did you really have to offer to kiss the poor man? He probably thinks you've got the hots for him now."

"Oooh! Come 'ere you beast," she replied, wrapping her husband in a bear hug. "You know you're the only man for me."

"Put me down, woman! You can't get all fluffy in a school."

Marcus Harris smiled to himself as he watched Lara's parents walk away hand in hand across the playground, with a small fuzzy dog trotting at their heels. He gathered together his books for his next class.

"I'll be back in forty minutes, Janice," he called on his way out.

Chapter Seven

When her dad arrived home, Lara was already busy in the workshop. The sharp sound of nails being hammered into wood rang out of the workshop door. He made two cups of tea and went to investigate. He watched his daughter's progress from the doorway, sipping his tea until the girl noticed him and stood back, removing her ear defenders.

"So it's nearly finished, then," he commented. "Let's have a look at it." He ran his hand over the smooth surface of the sofa seat admiringly. The cornflower-blue covering was almost complete; Lara had been hammering the last few edges into place. It had a fresh, soft feel that was pleasing.

"It's a good colour," Mr Frost murmured. "Will this fabric be easy to clean?"

"Yes. It's waterproof, so it won't attract bugs and it can be wiped down," replied Lara.

"A good choice, then," confirmed her dad. "Does the seat swing smoothly now?"

"Yes, I've re-oiled all the mechanisms and adjusted the buttons. It works perfectly."

Mr Frost's eyes glowed. "Lara, I am very proud of you!" he said, placing one hand on her shoulder. "This is really, really impressive."

Lara smiled shyly. "Thanks, Dad."

"Come on, I'll help you get the base fabric tacked on and then we can move it into the Quiet Room this evening." Father and daughter set to work again, happily navigating around

DOI: 10.4324/9781003208044-8

each other with little need for instruction or conversation. It was how they had operated since Lara was old enough to hold a screwdriver. As a small girl, Lara had spent hours in the workshop watching her dad saw, hammer and glue. It had seemed miraculous how he could turn a few pieces of wood into an exquisitely finished cabinet or chest of drawers. Lara had always loved the clean lines of the completed pieces and enjoyed running her hands down the smooth polished wood. All the chopping, sawing and measuring seemed logical to her, predictable and safe. She even found she could cope with the noise by wearing ear defenders, particularly as her dad always warned her when he was about to use loud machinery, so it was never a surprise. It was odd how school noises could make her panic, but the clatter of the workshop was comforting. Perhaps it was because she felt in control in the workshop. Lara wasn't sure; it was often hard to understand her own brain.

When Amelia was safely in bed two hours later, Lara, Teddy and their parents were all huffing and puffing like angry wolves as they negotiated the sofa through the kitchen and into the Quiet Room. With relief, they placed it down near the back wall, opposite the television. Pickle eyed the new sofa thoughtfully, wondering if he would be allowed to sit on it.

"Phew! Why didn't I marry a baker instead of a cabinet maker? Cakes are much easier to move around than sofas," panted Mrs Frost, flopping down on to Lara's new creation.

"Ah, but look how fit and strong all that furniture moving has made you," laughed her husband, squeezing her biceps. Teddy sidled over to his sister.

"Does it work?" he whispered.

"Of course it does," replied Lara, sounding slightly confused by the suggestion that it might not.

"Go on, then; make it eat Mum," whispered Teddy with a wicked grin. Lara looked slightly worried.

"Would it be OK?" she quizzed her brother.

"Yeah, she'll love it," lied Teddy. Lara felt in her pocket for the remote control. She looked at her mum, who was sitting comfortably on the sofa, smiling up at her dad. Lara pressed the large red button on the remote control. Suddenly, Mrs Frost's legs flew into the air showing a rather unusual pair of purple frilly knickers under her skirt. Before she had time to react, the seat and the back of the sofa flipped over and she disappeared from sight.

"Lara, you rotter," gasped her dad, before bursting out laughing. "Well, it certainly works! Are you all right, my love?"

"Lara Frost, just you wait until I get out of here!" squawked the sofa. Teddy was leaping up and down with delight.

"It might be safer to leave her in there," he whispered to Lara and then in a louder voice, "Nice pants, Mum."

"Oh Lord!" gasped the sofa. "Am I wearing the purple ones?"

"Yes!" replied her family in unison.

"They were the only ones I could find this morning. Auntie Mabel gave them to me for Christmas."

"Yes, we remember," her husband shouted back, clearly recalling his wife's horrified expression when she'd opened Auntie Mabel's package on Christmas Day, in front of four other elderly relatives.

"Do you know," came the voice from the sofa, "it's rather comfortable in here. I might just have a little snooze."

"Quick, let her out," breathed Teddy. "We need her to cook supper." Lara pressed the green button on the remote control and the sofa seat spun round again, depositing her mother back on the middle of the sofa. Her hair was a mess, and her skirt had ridden up her thighs, but she looked quite pleased with the experience.

"Hmm," said Mr Frost. "If you wear those knickers on that sofa again, I can strongly recommend trousers instead of a skirt."

"Oh dear," replied Mrs Frost, patting her skirt back into place. "Are they really that bad?"

"Yes!" was the unanimous reply.

By the time supper was ready, the whole family had been eaten and spat out by the sofa several times. Lara was buzzing with her success. The design worked perfectly. There were two ways to rotate the sofa seat, either using the remote control or by pressing a small button tucked out of sight between the seat and the sofa arm. The cavity in the body of the sofa was dark and soft like a cocoon. There were ventilation holes all down the back of the cavity so that breathing inside it was not a problem. There was a small button inside the cavity that would spin the sofa again, scooping up anyone inside and leaving them back on the seat. A small red light showed on the front leg when someone was hiding inside.

"Jeeeeeeepers," squeaked Teddy. "This is sooo cool. I can't wait to tell all my friends."

"Whoa! Hang on," said Mr Frost. "If this sofa is going to be helpful, we need to have some rules. Lara, are you listening?" Lara was so excited that she was spinning in circles with delight. "Right, calm down everyone and listen. The main purpose of this sofa is to give Lara a chance to disappear rather than have to talk to people if she is feeling stressed and needs some quiet time. It will only work if it is kept a secret."

"You know what Amelia was like when we suggested that Lara locked the door to this room when she needed quiet time," Mrs Frost reminded them. "Amelia just banged on the door whenever it was locked because she knew Lara was in here."

"So until Amelia and the twins are old enough to properly understand that Lara may need time on her own, we can't tell them about the sofa," Mr Frost explained. "I'm afraid, Teddy, that means that we can't tell anyone else either."

"Aw!" replied Teddy, drooping with disappointment.

"It's frustrating, but it's important."

Teddy nodded.

"Lara, if you are feeling too stressed to talk to people, press the button and you'll disappear into the sofa. If we come in and see that the red light is on, we'll know that you are inside and we'll take Amelia through to the kitchen. OK?" The children agreed.

"Can I use it when old people come to visit?" asked Lara.

Mrs Frost was the one to answer,

"You can't use it as an excuse to avoid all visitors who come to the house. It is just to be used to give you a few minutes' peace while you prepare yourself for meeting guests. Or to give you a chance to hide and then run up to your bedroom if the little ones are being really noisy."

"Is that understood?" confirmed Mr Frost. Both children nodded. "Great! Now can I have another go on it?" he asked, just as excited as his children.

Mrs Frost watched Lara spin her father in and out of the sofa several times. What her daughter had designed and created was incredible, and Mrs Frost's heart was bursting with pride. Whether Lara would be able to use it in the way that she hoped remained to be seen.

Chapter Eight

Dylan and Lara fell into the habit of eating their lunch together in the school vegetable patch, sitting on the grass with their backs pressed up against the fence. They talked or sat in comfortable silence. On one of the days, Dylan had brought another boy with him called Aryan.

"He's shy like me," explained Dylan to Lara. "I thought we could all be shy together."

"I'm not shy, I'm autistic," corrected Lara.

"What does that mean?" asked Aryan.

Lara thought for a bit. She didn't often try to explain autism to other people. Her brain was normal to her because that was how it had always been, although she was increasingly aware that her sense of normal was different from other people's normal.

Eventually, she said, "It means I'm not very good at talking to people, and for me lots of things are confusing."

"Hmm. It sounds like being shy," said Dylan.

"I don't think so," corrected Lara again. "My brain seems to work in a different way compared with everyone else's."

Aryan shrugged. "There's nothing wrong with being different," he said quietly.

"Yeah," agreed Dylan. "Let's be different together and eat our lunch out here. It's much nicer than the dining hall."

The others nodded in agreement.

DOI: 10.4324/9781003208044-9

The vegetable patch was in clear view of Mr Harris's office window, and he had watched the three pupils talking and settling on the grass to eat their lunch together. He drummed his fingers on the window ledge, pondering for a while, and then went to find Janice.

"Can you ask the caretaker to move a picnic table and benches round to the vegetable patch?"

"Of course, Mr Harris."

"Oh, and please ask Mrs Bloxham to come and see me. I'd like her to set up a new gardening club after lunch for some of the Year 7s." Janice scribbled down 'Bloxham', 'gardening club' and 'table' on her notepad so she didn't forget. Mr Harris wandered back to his office window and smiled at the three pairs of legs he could see sitting on the grass and the sound of laughter drifting from the vegetable garden.

Dylan smiled at Lara when he saw her in Maths a few days later. She took her normal seat by the wall, and Miss Fisher now knew better than to suggest that she moved. For Lara, the lesson was uneventful. She found Maths easy. Numbers were reliable. They never did anything unexpected. She was really excited about the next lesson.

For the first few weeks they had done art on a Wednesday morning, but today they would have their first DT lesson.

Designing and making things was Lara's passion. Her man-eating sofa was her most recent success. Before that, she had made a kennel for Pickle, helped build the treehouse and made her own desk for her bedroom. She loved being in her father's workshop with its neatly ordered tools and clear rules about how the equipment should be used. The smell of freshly sawn wood and polish was comforting. Lara expected the DT lab to feel similar. She would understand all the tools and techniques, so the lessons would be predictable and fun. She glanced at her timetable and noted that her teacher was called Mr Prendergast. She didn't think she had met him yet, but if he was calm and good-humoured like her father, she knew the lessons would be great. She was desperate to tell Mr Prendergast about her sofa.

The sofa had already hugely improved her life at home. On the night after they installed it, Lara had been watching a Bond film in the Quiet Room, when her younger sister and cousins had burst in through the front door. Lara had felt the usual panic as she heard them approach, chattering noisily in the corridor – and then she remembered the sofa. She pressed the button under the arm of the sofa and swooshed away into the dark, cosy compartment beneath the seat. Lara found the sudden movement temporarily disorientating, but she quickly recovered because she knew what was happening. Pickle, however, thought that the world had come to an end. One second he was sitting on Lara's lap, the next he was upside down in the dark, with his eyes popping out of his head and all four legs sticking up in the air like an overturned table. Luckily, he was a very peaceable creature by nature, and when Lara began gently stroking his tummy in the darkness, he gradually relaxed and nestled against the warmth of her side.

Amelia was the first into the Quiet Room, with the twins thundering in her wake, calling, "Lara! Lara! Lara!"

"No Lara," said Amelia, wandering around the empty room in surprise. James Bond was dashing across the television screen in the middle of a car chase. "Mummy, where's Lara?" Mrs Frost popped her head around the door and noted the red light was showing near the base of the sofa, so Lara must be inside. She turned off the TV.

"She's probably gone upstairs to do her homework. Best not to disturb her now. Go and play in the garden while I get you a snack." She then herded the three children through the kitchen and out into the garden beyond. Lara remained beneath the sofa, cuddling Pickle. It was warm, comfortable and dark. She felt peaceful and safe, in a cocoon of her own making. She smiled contentedly.

"Lara . . . Lara," called her mother softly. "You can come out now. The little ones are in the garden." Lara waited for a while, reluctant to re-emerge into the real world. "Lara, come on. Out you come," called her mother. In the dark, Lara felt for the button and pressed it firmly. Holding Pickle, she whooshed back on to the sofa seat. Pickle scrambled unsteadily to his feet and shook himself vigorously.

"Good gracious! Poor Pickle," exclaimed Mrs Frost. "How did he end up under there?"

"He was on my lap when I pressed the button," replied Lara. Pickle had already settled back on Lara's lap as if nothing had happened.

"Well, he doesn't seem to have minded," laughed her mother. "Now, head upstairs to your bedroom. I'll keep Amelia and the twins occupied down here so you get some peace."

"OK," Lara replied. Pickle trotted after her as she headed up the stairs.

Lara was beginning to find that she could cope with the little ones better, now that she was able to ensure that they didn't burst in on her. As her confidence grew, she would sometimes take Pickle out to join them in the garden while they had their snack.

There had only been one sofa disaster so far, which was when Granny Edith had come for tea. Lara decided that she couldn't face Granny Edith's powdery kiss that afternoon and so she pressed the button and disappeared beneath the sofa, just as her grandmother wandered into the Quiet Room, sipping a mug of tea.

"Gosh! What a splendid new sofa," remarked Granny Edith to Mrs Frost, as she emerged from the kitchen with the tea tray.

"Yes, it's super isn't it?" replied Mrs Frost, hastily adding, "Let's sit in the front room, Mum; we'll get the evening sun in there." Granny Edith took a sip from her mug and went across and stroked the cornflower-blue fabric of the sofa arm."

"It really is splendid; your Jimmy is very skilled."

"Actually, Lara made it, with only a little help from Jimmy."

"Oh my days! What a talented girl she is," exclaimed Granny Edith, turning to sit on the sofa. The sofa responded with a soft grumbling growl. Granny Edith's hearing was not good enough to hear the noise, but Mrs Frost's eyes widened. "It's extremely comfortable," continued Granny Edith, bouncing up and down on the sofa seat.

"I really think the front room would be best," said Mrs Frost persuasively, with just a hint of desperation in her voice. Granny Edith gave an extra-large bounce, which was unwise as she still held half a mug of tea. The sofa responded with a disgruntled growl and a scrabbling sound. Then, with no warning, Granny Edith's legs flew up into the air and she disappeared from sight, leaving Lara and Pickle lying on the sofa seat.

"Lara! Bring my mother back this instant!" Mrs Frost hissed furiously. Lara swiftly pressed the button under the sofa arm and whirled away with Pickle into the darkness, and Granny Edith returned to the sofa seat. There was a brief pause while Mrs Frost, still clutching the tea tray, stared at her mother in horror.

Granny Edith patted her hair with one hand and calmly remarked, "I'm so sorry, dear, I seem to have spilt my tea. I must have had a funny turn; everything went dark for a minute."

"How extraordinary, Mother," replied Mrs Frost smoothly, and then more briskly, "Never mind, these things happen. You look quite perky now. I'll top up your tea in the other room."

"Thank you, dear," replied Granny Edith, following along behind a little unsteadily.

Lara relaxed in the darkness with Pickle snuggled at her side. She made a mental note to make a cover for the button inside the sofa to prevent further accidents. The foam lining of the compartment gently pressed against her and she felt the stresses of the day slowly ebb away. She lay there in contented silence for some time until the sound of voices saying goodbyes filtered into her thoughts and the front door shut with a clunk. She pressed the button and swooshed back on to the sofa. Her mother came scurrying into the Quiet Room.

"Lara, really! That was an awful thing to do!" Lara was feeling so relaxed that she couldn't immediately focus on what she had done wrong. Then she remembered Granny Edith.

"I'm sorry. I'm sorry. Pickle pressed the button by mistake when he started wriggling."

Mrs Frost suddenly hooted with laughter. "Oh heavens, you should have seen her pants! They were pink and spotty and almost came down to her knees. I bet Auntie Mabel gave them to her."

Lara grinned shyly. "Sorry," she said again.

"Next time, just come and say hello to your grandmother," Mrs Frost chided. "Don't worry. I'll make sure she doesn't cover you in powdery kisses!" Laughing, she disappeared with the tea tray into the kitchen.

Chapter Nine

Lara and Dylan arrived at DT at the same time and sat next to each other in comfortable silence, but by the time the rest of the class had filed in, Lara was feeling on edge. The metal stools on which they sat made a terrible scraping sound against the stone floor. Every time a stool was moved, Lara winced as if in pain.

"Here comes Mr Prender-ghastly," whispered Dylan gloomily.

"Silence!" called the old person who had entered the class. Lara turned to examine her DT teacher and realised with deep disappointment that they had met before. He had told her off in the corridor the previous week when she had got lost and was late for a lesson. She often didn't recognise people whom she had only met once, but she would never forget this old person. The way he drew his thin lips back from his teeth in an unpleasant grimace reminded Lara of her neighbour's giant poodle, which often growled at her through the bars of its garden gate. He wasn't the type of old person that Lara expected to be a teacher. In fact, Lara thought he didn't look like a typical old person at all. He was too scruffy and had stains on his tie. She struggled to adjust her former expectations to the new reality.

"I am Mr Prendergast, your Design and Technology teacher," he whined. His voice was almost as unbearable to Lara's ears as the scraping stools. "Today we are going to start planning a pencil holder." The disappointment made

DOI: 10.4324/9781003208044-10

Lara slump in her seat. "You will spend the lesson drawing plans for your pencil pots, so everyone needs a pencil and a piece of paper." Lara wrestled with frustration. She had assumed that she would design and build something challenging in DT. Simply drawing a pencil pot was not what she had anticipated. She felt her hand starting to shake, which was never a good sign.

A pencil holder would be so simple, particularly with all the machinery available in the room. She looked around at the laser cutter, circular saws, jigsaws and all kinds of other equipment that she not only recognised but could operate blindfolded. Abruptly, the technical part of her mind started whirring as she began thinking how she could make the tedious 'pencil holder project' more interesting. Her brain flooded with images. She envisaged secret compartments, sliding doors and a switch that could fire elastic bands out of a chamber and into the air. Lara became totally absorbed in her ideas. She tuned out from Mr Prendergast's grumbling voice, the scraping stools and fluorescent lights of the DT lab, relishing the images in her mind.

"My biggest priority," continued Mr Prendergast, "is to ensure that all health and safety procedures are followed during these classes." Several pupils groaned and shifted around in their seats. "Therefore," droned the teacher, "no pupils will be allowed to use a machine until they have passed a health and safety test to show that they can operate it safely." The Year 7 pupils wilted as Mr Prendergast's negativity settled over them like a dense, wet fog. It smothered any remaining enthusiasm, replacing it with a dull apathy.

Dylan sighed, picking up his pencil and staring forlornly at a blank piece of paper.

"What are you going to do?" he asked Lara. "I bet you've got some good ideas."

"Yes, I have," she replied brightly. She began explaining her design, speaking rapidly about every detail without pausing for comment. Dylan smiled. He began sketching, listening with half his mind and drawing with the other half. He knew better than to interrupt Lara when she was excited about something.

"Wow, that sounds complicated!" he said when she finally paused. "I'm not very good at designing things, so mine will have to be a bit simpler."

Encouraged, Lara set to work on a very detailed drawing of her design, complete with instructions for how the pieces would fit together and the way in which all the moving parts worked. She began to enjoy herself.

As she was completely focused on the task, she didn't notice Mr Prendergast standing over her until his voice whined in her ear, "That will never work. It is far too complicated for a Year 7 project. You'd have to use a jigsaw to cut around all those corners and you don't have the skills to operate one. Start again."

Lara felt the blood pounding in her ears. She had a plan, a plan she knew she had the skills to complete. She looked up at the teacher. *What was the old person's name? Mr Poodle? No, that wasn't right. Mr Prender-ghastly. That was it.* She had to explain that she couldn't just abandon her idea and start again with something simple, something boring.

"It's a good plan, Mr Prender-ghastly. I can do it and I can use a jigsaw. I've just built a sofa," she explained in a rush.

"What did you call me?" snapped Mr Prendergast.

"Mr Prender-ghastly," replied Lara truthfully.

"Prendergast," cut in Dylan quickly. "She said Prendergast, Sir. Lara is very good at designing things but she finds it hard to remember teachers' names." Mr Prendergast eyed Dylan suspiciously before turning his attention back to Lara,

"And what's this rubbish about building a sofa?"

"It's a man-eating sofa," explained Lara, as though it was totally normal to have meat-eating furniture.

"Is that supposed to be funny?" the teacher retorted. "Because it's not. Sofas don't eat people."

"Mine does," insisted Lara.

"Honestly!" He rolled his eyes towards the ceiling as if his mother had just asked him to tidy his bedroom. "Young people today are so arrogant! This is only your first lesson and already you're too big for your boots."

Lara looked down at her feet, perplexed. "I'm not wearing boots."

"You know perfectly well what I mean," barked Mr Prendergast. "The children at this school get ruder every year," he moaned, losing interest in Lara and turning back to the class. He raised his voice and bellowed, so the whole class could hear, "Just so it is quite clear, no one in this class will be allowed to use the power tools until you have proved you can handle them competently." He moved away from Lara's table and launched into a general rant about young people being disrespectful.

"You can see why he is known as Mr Prender-ghastly," whispered Dylan, "but don't actually call him that again, Lara. He'll go bonkers." Lara wasn't listening. Her mind was focused on something else.

The children busied themselves with their pencil pot designs, keen not to be singled out for an undeserved rebuke. On and on whinged Mr Prendergast, without imparting any useful knowledge about how to design a pencil pot. The children bent lower over their pages, like a shoal of fish huddling together in the face of a prowling shark. Suddenly, Mr Prendergast snapped his head to the right, his attention drawn by the sound of a mechanical whirring.

Lara had decided to prove that she was able to work a jigsaw in the only way she knew how. She would demonstrate her skill to the old person and then he would see that she knew what she was doing and let her make her design. She had efficiently plugged in the tool, checked the blade, switched it on and begun cutting long, swooping waves in a thin piece of wood. Mr Prendergast was dumbstruck. He could not believe that Lara had defied him. Total fury swept across his face. Lara glanced up at him, but in her excitement, she failed to interpret her teacher's furious expression as a warning. She smiled at him, expecting him to share her enthusiasm and believing he would be impressed with her skill. Her classmates cautiously gathered round, keen to see what she had done, and Mr Prendergast's anger exploded across the small crowd of onlookers.

"How dare you defy me!" he shrieked. "Give that saw to me right now!" Lara's smile slowly faded. She was unable to comprehend his fury. She lifted the saw out of the wood and was suddenly not sure what to do with it. Her father always taught her to turn machinery off before passing it to anyone, but the old person was yelling at her and all the other children were pressing around her. Everything was happening too fast.

"I'm sorry. I'm sorry," she stammered. Her brain couldn't interpret all the sensations. For a moment, she was confused.

"Give me that saw this minute," the teacher screamed. So she held it out towards him, unfortunately presenting the moving blade towards his face. Mr Prendergast leapt back.

"Don't threaten me, you wicked child!" he screeched. "Put that saw down at once." Lara was pleased to receive a simple, clear instruction. She deftly turned off the saw and laid it on the workbench. She turned to Mr Prendergast,

"You see, Mr Old Person, I can work a jigsaw. In fact, I know how to use all the machines in here." Mr Prendergast was spluttering with rage.

"How dare you call me an old person. I'm only thirty-five," he cried. "How dare you use one of my power tools without my permission. Get out of my sight! Now!" Lara blinked several times, as though she had only just become aware of her surroundings. She stared at the faces crowding around her and began to shrink away from the torrent of fury pouring from the teacher's mouth. "Get out!" He spat at her, spraying a fine mist of saliva across the table. She stumbled, bumping into the workbench. Then she pushed through the other children and fled the workshop, leaving the door swinging behind her. "And don't come back!" bellowed Mr Prendergast into the silence that she left behind.

Dylan counted the minutes until the end of the lesson. He could not concentrate on his pencil pot design. It seemed rather pointless compared with the jigsaw incident. As soon as the lesson ended, he gathered his belongings and Lara's bag and dashed from the room. He headed straight for the vegetable garden and, sure enough, found Lara draped over the new picnic table. Her face was streaked with tears. They sat for a while looking at the green tops of the carrots and the bare patch of earth where the apple tree might show in time.

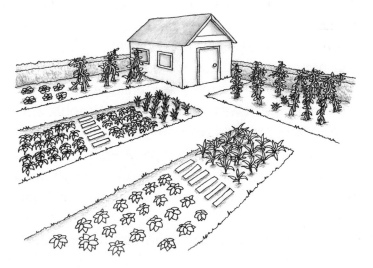

Eventually, Lara sighed,

"I like vegetables; they don't do anything surprising." Dylan nodded. "Why do I always make a mess of things? DT should have been my best lesson and it was a disaster."

"I think Mr Prender-ghastly is a disaster," replied Dylan kindly. "Grumpy gits like him shouldn't be allowed to teach." He smiled weakly at Lara, who stared at the carrots. "Have you really built a sofa?" he asked.

"Yes," replied Lara bleakly. "A man-eating one. Although I suppose it ought to be called a woman-eating sofa, because so far it's eaten more women than men."

"That sounds awesome," enthused Dylan. "How does it work?"

Lara began to explain, providing far more detail than was necessary as she became enthused by the topic. Dylan let her ramble, relieved that her mood was brightening.

"Your poor grandmother! I can't believe you tipped her under the sofa," Dylan said at last.

"I didn't mean to. It was Pickle who pressed the button. Granny Edith's tea made an awful mess of the compartment underneath. It took ages to mop up," replied Lara.

Dylan grinned. "May I see it sometime?" Lara thought about this. She didn't usually ask children from school to come to her home. It was easier if school people stayed at school and family friends were at home.

"All right," she said, "but only if you keep it a secret." Lara shivered in the morning breeze. "Dylan . . . what does 'Too big for your boots' mean? I wasn't even wearing boots."

Dylan laughed.

"Come on," he replied. "We'll talk about it over lunch."

Marcus Harris felt tired and slightly sick. He sat very still, absorbing the fury that was being hurled across the desk at him. He was trying to remember if Eric Prendergast had ever said anything nice about anyone, but it was hard to think with the DT teacher ranting at him.

"I will not teach a child who is deliberately rude and disobedient," raved Mr Prendergast, spraying spit on to Mr Harris's in-tray. Mr Harris suspected that Lara would give a very different account of the incident. "That girl tried to cut me with a jigsaw. She's a menace." Mr Prendergast emphasised the next sentence by repeatedly jabbing the headteacher in the chest with his bony index finger. "She is never setting foot in my workshop again!"

On the final jab, Mr Harris stood and swept the larger man's hand to one side. "Sit down!" he ordered in a commanding tone. Mr Prendergast shuffled back and sat on the sofa like an obedient terrier waiting to be disciplined. Even in his fury, he perhaps realised that chest-prodding the headteacher was a step too far. Marcus Harris stood looking down at Mr Prendergast in frustration. Finally, he spoke. "Eric, I am fed up with you shouting at me several times a week about the poor behaviour of students in your classes. I appreciate that teaching can be challenging, but the students are generally well behaved in this school."

"Well, that Frost girl isn't! She's a disgrace," shot back Mr Prendergast.

Mr Harris sighed. "Eric, Lara is a bright girl but she often makes social errors. She is autistic and so needs our support to succeed in school. I expect **all** teachers to make reasonable adjustments to support children with special educational needs."

"It's still no excuse for attacking me with an electric saw," countered Mr Prendergast petulantly.

"Possibly not, but in my experience, Lara's behaviour always has a logic if you just take time to understand the situation from her point of view." Mr Harris took a deep breath. "And another thing, your angry outbursts have got to stop. As teachers, it is our job to be good role models for our pupils."

Mr Prendergast was too busy being angry to focus on his own appalling behaviour. "You'd better exclude her or I'll complain to the Governors," he growled.

"As headteacher of this school, **I** shall decide whether Lara Frost should be disciplined or not, but I shall certainly speak to the Governors about whether you should remain in your job."

"You wouldn't dare sack me," stated Mr Prendergast. "I'd sue you for unfair dismissal."

"If there is evidence that your behaviour is having a negative impact on the pupils of this school, I most certainly will ask you to leave, Eric. I will no longer tolerate you shouting at me, my staff or the pupils." Mr Harris sat down and began tidying his papers to indicate that the meeting had come to an end. His bushy eyebrows were quivering with emotion. "Now take some deep breaths and control yourself. You need to return to class for your next lesson."

Eric Prendergast retreated towards the door, muttering, "You wouldn't dare sack me."

"Yes, Eric, I would," replied Mr Harris.

Mr Prendergast slunk out, ignoring Janice in the outer office, and disappeared into the corridor. Standing up, Mr Harris moved over to the window, taking deep breaths to steady his nerves. He hated arguments. His hands trembled where they lay on the window ledge. Janice appeared quietly next to him and handed him a steaming cup of tea.

"Bravo, Mr Harris," she said.

"Did I do all right?" he asked humbly.

"You were magnificent," she replied.

They sipped their tea, standing companionably side by side. Janice pointed to the five pupils who were finishing their lunch, sitting at the new picnic table by the vegetable garden.

"Look, Mr Harris," she said. "It's Lara."

Mr Harris followed her gaze and saw Lara sitting with four other pupils. He recognised Dylan and a boy called Aryan, and there were two other girls who had their backs to him. It was clear that the pupils were chatting, and Lara was laughing. He'd never seen her laugh before. She had a beautiful smile. Mrs Bloxham was striding over towards the group. She called to them as she approached.

"Greetings, my fellow gardeners!" She placed a basket of seeds on the table. "What shall we plant today?" The five pupils gathered around her, chatting, smiling and all making suggestions. Janice turned to Mr Harris.

"It makes it all worth it, to see them happy like that," she said.

"Yes. It most certainly does," he replied.

Chapter Ten

On the day of the accident, Marcus Harris was tired but in a typically good mood. He unlocked his bicycle and turned up his collar against the evening chill. It was late. He had been helping out at the Computer Club which ran on Tuesday evenings. Lara Frost had been there, and he had enjoyed seeing her lead the group's coding task and helping out other pupils who found it more difficult than she did.

It had been a couple of weeks since he had spoken to the school staff and explained Lara's needs. Eric Prendergast had been typically negative, but the rest of the teachers were wonderful. They were open to putting strategies in place for Lara. Miss Fisher confided after the meeting that she now understood Lara's unfortunate comments about her bottom. She had a very forgiving nature at heart. Mr Thornhill had agreed with Lara's observation that the stools in the Art and DT rooms made a terrible scraping noise on the stone floors, and everyone decided that it would help the tolerance of both staff and pupils if rubber feet were fitted to the stools to make them quieter. Janice was looking into the cost of rubber feet. Mr Harris could see the money he had carefully saved to replace the sofa in his office was probably going to be spent on rubber feet instead. *Ho hum, such is life*, he thought to himself.

The good news was that Lara had only been sent to him once in the last week, which indicated that things must be going better for her at school. That hadn't stopped Eric

 DOI: 10.4324/9781003208044-11

Prendergast complaining about her. It was almost as though the teacher was seeking the girl out to find fault with her. Mr Harris banished all thoughts of Eric Prendergast from his mind as he mounted his bike, relishing the exercise on his way home. He passed Mr Thornhill as he left the car park.

"Goodnight, Marcus," called Mr Thornhill, "Aren't you going the wrong way?"

"Just popping to the shops before going home. I'll be cycling back this way in a minute."

"Well, go carefully. It's a strangely gloomy night."

"I will," replied Mr Harris. "Oh – great Computer Club tonight, Robert," he called over his shoulder.

"Yes, they're a good bunch of kids," replied Mr Thornhill. "Good night, Marcus. See you tomorrow."

It was true – Lara was having a good week. Being allowed to wear earplugs or headphones when school was noisy made life much less stressful. She could still hear what the teacher said, but the noise was muffled enough for her to ignore many of the irritating sounds that set her teeth on edge. She and Dylan, along with a few others, had lunch together most days, usually in the vegetable garden. Lara really liked Mrs Bloxham's Gardening Club. Mr Harris had suggested she joined the Computer Club, which she had just attended. She was late walking home because she had stayed behind talking to some of the Year 9 pupils about ideas for a new computer program that they hoped to design. It had been a busy day but good. She put on her headphones, playing some music to drown out the noise of the world. Her mind was buzzing with all her ideas from Computer Club so she settled herself by focusing on the plodding rhythm of her feet, walking on the squares to avoid the bears. *Plod, plod, walk on the squares to avoid the bears*, she chanted to herself.

Mr Harris heard the car before he saw it. He was cycling down a residential street next to the park, which had little traffic at this time of night. It was a curiously dismal evening, the air thick with a foggy drizzle. It was lucky his wife had insisted he take his bike lights and reflective jacket to school with him that morning because it was quite hard to see along the street. Ahead of him was the zebra crossing. He dimly saw a figure in a dark coat, hood pulled up against the rain, marching down the pavement towards the crossing. The figure was plodding purposefully but with a slightly strange gait. It swayed a little from side to side and every now and then took an extra-large or extra-small step. He laughed to himself. It must be Lara walking home, avoiding the bears. She had told him about the bears and having to keep to the squares. He peddled closer to the crossing. He could see the car now, coming fast towards him on the other side of the road. The figure was about the step on to the crossing without looking at the road. It was as if the girl knew that she had right of way on a zebra crossing and so didn't need to check for cars. Had she not heard the car? Mr Harris could see that it was accelerating towards the crossing. Had the driver not seen the child? It would surely slow down any second. But he realised it was going faster still. He pedalled more rapidly – he had to warn Lara.

"Watch out!" he yelled, but the figure did not respond. Lara was cocooned in her own world of music beneath the hood of her coat.

Mr Harris could see the driver now and hear the music thumping out of the car windows. He saw a well-dressed young man in the driver's seat. His phone was clasped under his chin and he was gesturing wildly with his right hand. It was clear that the driver had not noticed the girl or the crossing, which were fast approaching. Mr Harris desperately pedalled harder. He was about to witness the death of a child and there seemed to be nothing he could do to prevent it.

"Lara, watch out!" he yelled again, but it was hopeless.

Before he had time to think, his instincts took over. He powered over the crossing and swerved into the path of the speeding car, placing himself between the car and the girl. There was a terrible screech of brakes and he felt himself catapult over the handlebars of his bike and land with a sickening crunch – then nothing.

Lara stood paralysed on the zebra crossing, trying to work out what had just happened. It was as though both the car and the cyclist had appeared from nowhere. There was screeching and then a bright yellow jacket flying through the air. What had happened? It must be her fault – these things always seemed to be her fault. She could hear rushing in her ears, and she wanted to sit down but didn't seem to be able to move. The driver's door of the car flew open and a young man leapt out.

"Oh my God! Oh my God! Oh my God!" he shouted, putting his hands up to his head. "I hit him. I didn't see him," he stammered, staring at Lara with wild eyes. "I didn't see you!"

Lara gazed at the young man in silence. *I knew it was my fault*, she thought. *I've killed a cyclist and I didn't even know he was there.* The young man rushed over to the side of the road towards the crumpled yellow jacket. He reached over the slumped body, gently feeling for a pulse.

"Can you hear me?" he called. "I'm getting help." After a few seconds, Lara heard, "Ambulance, please, to Fredrick Avenue. A cyclist has been hit. Please be quick!"

A woman ran towards the scene, drawn by the car abandoned in the road with the twisted frame of a bicycle beneath its wheels.

"Can I help?" she asked breathlessly.

"I think I've killed him," choked the driver.

The woman bent over the crumpled form, suddenly recognising his rucksack which had *MARCUS HARRIS* written in large letters across the back.

"Oh no! No! No! It's Mr Harris . . . Marcus, Marcus can you hear me? It's Louisa, Louisa Fisher from school." The body did not respond.

"Marcus, hang in there," commanded Miss Fisher. "An ambulance is on its way." His body lay half buried in bin bags that had been put out for collection the following morning. She began shoving the bags aside, gently trying to turn him over so she could see his face. "Marcus, please!" she pleaded desperately. "You've got to be OK."

"Louisa?" came a muffled voice. "Everything hurts. Please get this bag off my head, it stinks of rotting fish."

An ambulance and the police came. Mr Harris was carefully laid on a stretcher and carried away.

"Will he be OK?" Miss Fisher asked one of the ambulance crew.

"He's got a broken arm and a sore head. Lucky he was wearing his cycling helmet and landed in those bin bags, or it would have been a lot worse."

"Thank goodness," breathed Miss Fisher. "I'll call his wife and ask her to meet you at the hospital."

A voice began calling from the ambulance. "Louisa! Louisa! Where's Lara?" Miss Fisher poked her head into the back of the ambulance where Mr Harris was desperately trying to communicate with her.

"Lara . . . Lara Frost . . . she was on the crossing. Is she OK?"

"I've not seen her, Marcus. But don't worry, I'll find her," Miss Fisher replied.

The police took the driver away for questioning, although there was no need. He was sobbing his story over and over again. "It's my fault, I was on the phone. I didn't see the girl on the crossing until the cyclist pulled out in front of me. I would have killed her!"

"All right, Sir, let's get you down to the station," replied the policeman.

Lara sat in the shadows on the other side of the road, her back pressed against a tree. Her knees were drawn up to her chin and she was rocking backwards and forwards, not knowing what to do. She ought to tell one of the old people that it was her fault but she didn't know where to start. The fog was seeping through her jacket and the chilled pavement was gradually numbing her buttocks. She ought to be at home – but how could she explain to her parents that she had killed Mr Harris?

"Lara?" came a soft voice by her shoulder. "Lara, it's me, Miss Fisher. Are you OK?" Lara continued rocking.

"I'm sorry. I'm sorry, I'm sorry. I've killed Mr Harris. Mr Harris is dead," she murmured again and again into the evening air.

"Lara, Mr Harris is OK. You've had quite a shock. But it's all going to be fine." Lara didn't respond. Miss Fisher bent down on her knees in front of Lara, peering at the ashen face that was half hidden by the hood of the girl's coat.

"Lara, listen to me." She waited for the girl's eyes to gradually focus on her before continuing. "Mr Harris is alive. He's going to be OK." Miss Fisher waited until Lara began rocking more slowly and her breathing was steady, then she continued, "I'm going to take you home now. Can you show me the way?" Lara nodded and pointed up the street. Miss Fisher took her arm and gently led her home.

Both Mr and Mrs Frost opened the door when the doorbell rang. Pickle rushed out to welcome Lara, and she gathered him in her arms, deriving comfort from his warm furry body.

"Oh poppet, thank goodness. We were so worried. Are you all right, love?" Mrs Frost asked, taking in her white face and shaking hands.

"Mr and Mrs Frost? Hello, I'm Louisa Fisher, Lara's Maths teacher. I'm afraid there was a traffic accident when Lara was crossing the road. Please reassure her that she has done nothing wrong. She was using the zebra crossing and a driver obviously did not see her in the dark and sped towards the crossing without looking. By chance, Mr Harris was cycling home and managed to stop the car by pulling out in front of it on his bicycle.

"Good Lord!" cried Mr Frost. "Is he OK?"

"He has a broken arm but should be fine. It has been a nasty episode, but I'm sure that there will be no lasting damage once his arm mends. Lara will probably need a hot drink and to sit down for a while."

"Thank you so much for bringing her home, Miss Fisher."

"I'm just glad I was there and able to help. Goodnight."

As Miss Fisher reached the garden gate, Lara turned and called out, "Miss Fisher! Did Mr Harris save my life tonight?"

Miss Fisher thought for a moment and then replied, "Yes, Lara. I think he did."

Chapter Eleven

Lara was unusually quiet at breakfast the next day. She did not seem to notice Amelia's chatter as she slowly chewed her way through toast and marmalade, which she liked to have every weekday. Finally, she said, "Mum, when someone saves your life, what should you do?"

"What do you mean, Lara?" asked her mother.

"I've been thinking about it. Mr Harris deliberately put himself in danger, just to save me. That is a really big thing. I don't know what to do about it. Should I say thank you?"

"Yes, Lara, I think he would really appreciate that. It would be the right thing to do. Perhaps it would be good to give him a present as well, to show how grateful we are," suggested Mrs Frost. Lara's heart sank. She was hopeless at giving presents. She never knew what to choose.

"But what do I give him?" asked Lara.

Mrs Frost was about to suggest a box of chocolates but decided against it. Lara needed to start becoming more independent about making such decisions, rather than just doing what her mother suggested. She thought for a bit before replying.

"Lara, I think you should be the one to choose something. The present does not need to be expensive, but it should show that you have really thought about what the other person would like. Think of something that you would find special if someone gave it to you – then try to imagine what

DOI: 10.4324/9781003208044-12

Mr Harris would think was a special present. You are good at making things – perhaps you could make him something."

Lara sighed with the weight of the decision. It would have been so much easier if her mother had just told her what to give Mr Harris.

Lara pondered the problem all day until suddenly in the middle of a Chemistry lesson she found the answer – the man-eating sofa. It was her most special possession and a fair exchange for saving her life. Also, Mr Harris's sofa was awful and so it was clear that he would like a new one. Lara knew that she would miss the sofa terribly at home, but she could probably make another one. With her mind made up, she felt positively light-hearted for the rest of the afternoon until she encountered Mr Prendergast in the corridor.

Lara had struggled in the last few DT lessons. Mr Prendergast had said that she could only be in the room if she did not use any of the tools. It had taken three weeks for him to allow Lara to use a hand saw. The lessons were a complete waste of her time, but at least now that the stools had rubber feet and she was allowed to wear ear defenders, the sessions had become tolerable for her ears. The problem was that Mr Prendergast seemed to appear around every corner and always found fault with her. He materialised in front of her now, barring her way.

"Your shirt is untucked," he said, looking her up and down with a critical eye. Lara swiftly glanced up the corridor at the other pupils.

"Everyone's shirts are untucked," she replied reasonably.

"Don't answer me back, you scruffy girl. You're even wearing odd socks," the teacher snorted. "Have you no pride in your appearance?"

Lara thought for a while. She rarely paid any attention to what she wore, as long as it was comfortable. Her mother insisted that she had her hair cut from time to time, but that didn't give her any pride. So she gave an honest answer. "No."

"What!" bellowed the teacher. "You represent the school when you wear that uniform! How dare you not take pride in representing the school?"

As Lara didn't know how to answer the question, she said nothing. She peered at the other pupils who were filing past in the corridor. They all looked like her. Their uniforms were fine except that they all had their shirts untucked. She glanced back at Mr Prendergast, noticing his greasy hair, brown suit, dirty beige jumper and his tie that showed several stains. "I think you're scruffier than I am," she replied matter-of-factly.

Mr Prendergast grabbed Lara by the strap of her rucksack and dragged her along the corridor, past the dining hall and up towards the headteacher's office. Pupils parted to left and right to let them through, staring at Lara, generally with sympathy. None of them wanted to be singled out by Mr Prender-ghastly and they were grateful not to be in Lara's situation . . . all except one.

Julia Smythe smirked with delight as she saw Lara being dragged up the corridor by the furious teacher. Julia had not forgiven Lara for the humiliating episode in the dining hall and regularly found opportunities for petty revenge. She had done classic tricks such as taping *Kick the Geek* to Lara's back, as well as hiding her textbooks and PE kit, so that Lara was often in trouble for losing her belongings. However, now that Lara had friends, these techniques were becoming less effective. If Julia taped an insult to Lara's back, Dylan or Aryan would discreetly remove it. When Julia hid Lara's books, often someone would find and return them. With her efforts at revenge being continually frustrated, Julia's venom towards Lara was growing as time passed.

This time, Julia's vengeance was simple but effective. As Lara scurried by, struggling to keep her balance with Mr Prendergast tugging at her rucksack, Julia stuck out her foot. Lara tripped and fell headlong into Mr Prendergast. Like a falling domino, Mr Prendergast toppled to the ground with a splat, with Lara tangled in his ankles. The teacher was unusually silent and pupils filled the passage, gazing nervously at the two fallen bodies. The air had been knocked out of Mr Prendergast's lungs when he landed, and as he gasped for breath, he was filled with an outrage and fury like none he had ever felt before. He rose, lifted Lara to her feet and propelled her through the door to Janice's office. He dumped her on a chair and burst into Mr Harris's office. Janice glanced at Lara with concern and stood bracing herself for whatever Mr Prendergast had to say.

"I need to speak to Marcus NOW!" screeched the teacher.

"He is still in hospital after his accident last night," replied Janice calmly.

Mr Prendergast was momentarily caught off balance. He'd forgotten about the accident. He was so accustomed to shouting at the headteacher whenever he was angry that now he didn't know what to do in Mr Harris's absence. Then he narrowed his eyes and turned back to Lara. She was sitting, head down, with her arms wrapped around herself.

"I'm sorry. I'm sorry. I'm sorry," she chanted again and again towards the carpet.

"You! This is your fault!" he spat. "Mr Harris is injured because of you." He towered over the girl, and Janice moved quickly. She shot round her desk and placed herself between Lara and the snarling teacher. She was quite a small woman, but she did what she knew Mr Harris would have expected of her.

"Get out of my office, you bully," she hissed at Mr Prendergast, "or I'll call the police."

The teacher's eyes widened in shock, and he stood facing Janice for a lingering moment, clenching his fists. After a long, dangerous silence, he stepped back and, with a poisonous leer, snarled, "This won't be the end of the matter! You mark my words!" Then he turned and left the office, slamming the door on his way out.

Janice released her breath. She sat down heavily beside Lara and took her hand. Both of them were shaking.

"Tea," she said decisively. "We both need a cup of tea." With no warning, Lara burst into tears. The shock of the accident the previous day, combined with Mr Prendergast's rage, suddenly overwhelmed her. Janice sat beside her. She longed to wrap the girl in her arms to comfort her, but she knew that Lara might find this too intense. Instead, she reached for the box of tissues and sat peacefully by Lara's side, murmuring comforting words and waiting for the sobs to subside.

Finally, Lara gasped, "It's all my fault. Mr Harris could have been killed."

"Lara, it is not your fault," Janice explained gently. "You were on a zebra crossing. You had right of way. The man driving the car is the one who was at fault. It was his job to be looking where he was going and his job to stop for pedestrians. The only mistake you made was to assume that all drivers will follow the rules of the road. In future, always check for cars before you step on to a crossing."

"But Mr Harris could have been killed," choked Lara, "and he's always been so kind to me."

Janice smiled. "Mr Harris is a kind man and he likes you very much, Lara. But he threw himself in front of that car because he felt it was the right thing to do. He would have done the same for any pupil in this school."

"Really?"

"Definitely," Janice replied. Lara blew her nose noisily and the kettle came to the boil.

"Tea," said Janice again, "and we both need a chocolate biscuit."

The warming tea made both of them feel a little steadier. Lara had been staring at Janice's feet for some time. After a while, she said, "Miss, you're wearing odd shoes. One's red and the other's blue."

"I know," sighed Janice. "My puppy ate the left one from the blue pair and the right one from the red pair."

Lara thought about this for a while. "I don't think old people usually wear odd shoes," she observed. "Would it be best to buy a new pair?"

"Indeed, it would, Lara," replied Janice, who had become accustomed to Lara calling people 'old', "but unfortunately I'm short of money at the moment." Lara glanced fleetingly at Janice with large, concerned eyes. "My husband, Stan, has been ill for a while and hasn't been able to work. So for the time being, there's no spare money for new shoes."

"Oh," said Lara.

"At least the puppy's keeping Stan company while I'm at work," said Janice more brightly.

"I think that new green shoes would be nice," said Lara thoughtfully.

"Hmm, green. I've never had a pair of green shoes before," replied Janice.

Lara pondered for a while. Her mind was racing through images of green shoes, imagining how the leather would be cut and attached to the sole.

After some time, she looked up from the plate of biscuit crumbs and said, "I'm going to bring a sofa to school tomorrow."

"Oh?" said Janice. "Why's that?"

"I need to thank Mr Harris for saving my life and I have decided to give him the sofa I've made, as a thank-you present."

Janice frowned slightly as she thought of all the strange objects that Year 7 pupils produced in the DT department. She wondered if the new sofa might be worse than Mr Harris's revolting old one. But Lara was staring at her with total sincerity, and Janice decided that this was not the time to doubt her.

"Lara, I think that it is a lovely idea. I'll ask the caretaker to help me move the old one into the storeroom so that you can put your new one in Mr Harris's office. I don't think he will be back tomorrow, but it will be a wonderful surprise when he comes back to school."

Lara smiled and finished her tea.

Chapter Twelve

Mrs Frost was horrified when Lara related her encounter with Mr Prendergast.

"That man is not fit to be a teacher!" she exclaimed. "We will have to complain to Mr Harris when he has recovered." She was even more distraught when Lara said she was going to give away the sofa. "But, Lara, it took you months to make that sofa. I imagined that you might make Mr Harris a box, or a shelf for his papers or something. I'm sure he wouldn't expect you to give away your sofa. It means so much to you."

"It's OK, Mum, I've made up my mind. He needs a new sofa and I have one that I ought to give him. I can probably make another one. At least it means that whenever I get sent to his office, I won't have to sit on the old one. I can't bear the feel of it."

The decision was made, so the following morning the Frosts heaved the sofa into Mr Frost's furniture truck. With a bit of help, Lara and Mr Frost carried the sofa through the school reception to the headteacher's office. Pickle lay on the sofa seat, assuming that he was in charge of the whole operation.

DOI: 10.4324/9781003208044-13

"Wow! Lara, that is awesome," exclaimed Janice. "I am sure Mr Harris will be delighted. Thank you so much. He is due back tomorrow."

Lara looked fondly at the sofa. She went over and laid a thank-you card and the remote control on Mr Harris's desk. With a last look at her greatest achievement, she scooped Pickle up in her arms and left the office.

On the way out, Mr Frost clasped his daughter by the shoulder. "Well done, you," he commented. "I'm very proud of you this morning. Have a good day." He turned to wave to her as he left the building with Pickle trotting at his heels.

On his return to school, Mr Harris was still tired and sore. He was not meant to be back at work for a week, but he decided to pop in to check that all was well in his absence. Janice greeted him as he entered her outer office.

"Mr Harris! How lovely to see you, but you ought to be resting."

"I will, Janice, don't worry. I just came in to put a few things in order and then I'll head home again." He opened the door to his office and was immediately struck by the sight of a stunning cornflower-blue sofa, brand new and sparklingly clean.

"Janice! Where on earth did this sofa come from? It's wonderful!"

Janice smiled, peering over his shoulder. "I knew you'd like it. Mr Frost and Lara brought it in this morning. Lara made it herself! It's her way of saying thank you for saving her the other night."

"Goodness! How splendid! Although this is too generous. Did Lara really make it?"

"It appears so. Mr Frost said he hardly helped at all. It was Lara's design and nearly all her own work."

"It is astounding and immensely kind. I must find her to say thank you before I leave."

"That would be nice. I'm afraid there was a nasty incident with Lara and Mr Prendergast yesterday. I had to intervene when I thought the man was going to strike her."

"Oh no! Janice, will you write down all the details for me. That hateful man has got to go – and soon. I've just got to work out how."

Mr Harris settled at his desk and began working through the most urgent paperwork. He found a card from Lara which he put into his bag to open at home. There was also a remote control. He didn't understand where the remote control had come from. It had two big buttons, one red and the other green. Perhaps one of the teachers had confiscated it from a pupil.

He had only been at his desk for ten minutes when he heard Mr Prendergast stomp into the outer office. Janice clearly said that Mr Harris was not to be disturbed, but that did not stop the DT teacher from barging into the room.

"I've been waiting for you to get back," snarled the teacher, not offering a single comment of concern, despite Mr Harris's appearance. His right arm was in a sling, he had a nasty cut on his forehead and extensive grazing down one cheek as well as a terrible black eye. But Mr Prendergast was so absorbed in his own complaints that he had ceased to think about other people's problems. He was determined to have his daily moan and slouched on the sofa, grumbling about the shabby appearance of the pupils and that they were always late for his lessons.

Mr Harris was just too tired to argue. He was collecting evidence to have Mr Prendergast dismissed. The headteacher took in his colleague's shabby brown suit and stained tie. He tried hard not to judge people by their appearance, but he wished the man would at least wash his clothes. As Mr Prendergast's list of complaints continued to flow, Mr Harris became increasingly distracted. The painkillers he was taking were making it hard for him to concentrate. The remote control on his desk caught his eye. Those two big buttons were just begging to be pressed. Just for fun, he pressed the green button. Nothing happened. *It must be for some toy that is out of range*, he thought. For good measure, he pressed the red button. Immediately, Mr Prendergast's legs swung into the air and then with a swoosh he disappeared from view completely. Everything looked normal except that Mr Prendergast had gone. Marcus Harris stared incredulously at the sofa, wondering if he had taken too many painkillers that morning. But no – a muttering sound was coming from the sofa. He quickly grabbed Lara's card from his bag and tore open the envelope.

Dear Mr Harris,

Thank you for saving my life. I am very grateful and so have given you the thing that is most special to me. It is a man-eating sofa that I made with my dad. I hope you like it.

Warm wishes,
Lara.

Mr Harris roared with laughter until his bruised ribs hurt and tears poured from his eyes. Janice poked her head around the door to see what was going on.

"Oh, Janice," giggled Mr Harris. "This is wonderful. The sofa has just eaten Mr Prendergast."

Janice glanced at the empty sofa, thinking that Mr Harris had definitely come back to work too soon, when the sofa screeched, "Oi! What's going on? It's all dark in here!"

Janice looked at Mr Harris in amazement and then howled with laughter as well. It took them both quite a while to recover enough to be sensible. The process was not helped by a stream of obscenities from the sofa. Mr Harris repeatedly pressed the green and red buttons on the remote control, but nothing happened.

"Aha! Oh dear, oh dear, this won't do," spluttered Mr Harris. "Be an angel, Janice, and look up what lesson Lara is in. The problem is, I don't know how to get the old codger out again."

"Who are you calling an old codger? I'm younger than you," yelled the sofa.

"Well, you ought to ruddy well behave as though you are," shouted back Mr Harris, before dissolving into more laughter.

Lara hesitated outside Mr Harris's office. Janice had explained that the sofa has eaten Mr Prendergast. This was worrying, and when she heard him bellowing like a herd of distressed cows, her instinct was to run and hide. The feeling intensified when she caught sight of Mr Harris's battered and scuffed face, and a wave of guilt mingled with her feelings of terror.

Janice gently pushed her through the door to the inner office, saying, "It's all right; he's still yelling insults so he must be OK."

Mr Harris beamed when he saw Lara.

"Lara! What a fabulous surprise. I am delighted with the new sofa!" he called above the shrieking and thumping that filled the room. The sofa's language seemed to be getting worse and worse. Lara made a mental note of several words she did not recognise. She would have to ask Dylan what they meant.

"The only problem is," continued Mr Harris, "that the sofa seems to have eaten Mr Prendergast and I'm not sure how to get him out."

"The green button should release him," said Lara warily, thinking that it would be safest to leave Mr Prendergast where he was.

"I tried that but nothing happened."

"Oh, I think Dad dropped the remote when we were moving the sofa yesterday. I wonder if it has a loose connection?" Lara replied.

"Is there another way?" asked Mr Harris.

"There's a button by the left arm," explained Lara. Mr Harris and Janice waited for Lara to step forward and press the button, but she didn't move. The sofa was twitching and howling with rage.

"I think you'd better do it, Mr Harris," said Lara, looking absolutely terrified.

"Oh no, you don't – not with a broken arm," said Janice decisively. She stepped forward, felt around for the button, pressed it firmly and leapt back to a safe distance. With a tremendous whoosh, Mr Prendergast emerged and landed sprawled on the sofa seat. He was so angry he looked like a boiled beetroot. He tried to sit up, but his tie had become tangled in the seat mechanism, so he was attached to the sofa seat like a dog straining on a short lead. It took a moment for his eyes to focus on Lara, as he had to tilt his head up awkwardly to see the other people in the room. He began choking with rage, beating his fists on the seat like a toddler having a tantrum.

"You!" he yelled, pointing a quivering finger towards Lara's face. "You! I should have known that this would be your fault."

"Actually, Eric, I should take the blame," admitted Mr Harris, "I was the one who pressed the button."

"Get me out of here," wailed Mr Prendergast. "I'm being held hostage by the furniture." Mr Harris was unable to help. He had slumped down in his chair and was bellowing with laughter, using his good arm to clutch at his poor broken ribs. Janice swiftly took charge.

"Don't worry Mr Prendergast, we'll have you out of here in a jiffy," she said, reaching across Lara and taking a pair of scissors from the drawer of Mr Harris's desk. With a swift lunge, she cut Mr Prendergast's tie in two, allowing him to bob up into a seated position. He looked down at the stump of his tie that poked out of his shirt collar, and then at the other end that was trapped in the sofa seat like the tail of a mangy animal. His mouth fell open, but no words came out. Lara hid behind Janice.

Mr Harris was still unable to speak. He was sobbing with laughter; great streams of tears were pouring down his battered cheeks. He rocked backwards and forwards, thumping his desk with his good arm to emphasise his amusement.

Mr Prendergast blinked several times, then raised his chin and drew his shoulders back in an attempt to regain some dignity.

"I have never, never been so insulted in my life! No amount of money would persuade me to teach another lesson in this school."

Mr Harris instantly recovered his composure and swiftly replied, "Well, I'm very sorry to hear that, Eric. This business with the sofa was an unfortunate mistake. But I completely respect your decision to resign. Mr Thornhill will help you clear out your office so that you can leave by lunchtime." Mr Prendergast gaped at him. "I won't delay you further," the headteacher continued. "You'll need time to pack up. I will, of course, be happy to pay for the damage done to your tie."

Before Mr Prendergast could comprehend what had just happened, Janice guided him out through her office and into the corridor. He considered going back in to complain further but decided against it, due to the peals of laughter coming from within.

Lara stood awkwardly as Mr Harris dried his eyes and Janice tried to steady herself with deep breathing.

"I'm so sorry, Mr Harris. I didn't mean to make Mr Prendergast so angry. Is it a problem that he has resigned?"

"No, Lara, it is wonderful news. He was an awful teacher, and I was trying to think how I could ask him to leave without him making too much fuss. Your sofa was the perfect solution. What's more, it has cheered me up no end!"

Chapter Thirteen

Mr Harris returned to school the following week, still a little bruised but in high spirits. Mr Prendergast had left in a flurry. It meant that they were short-staffed, but the atmosphere in the staffroom was positively joyous without him there complaining about everything. It was such a relief not having to tolerate the cloud of angry gloom that had followed Mr Prendergast around the school.

Soon after his return, Mr Harris asked Mr Thornhill to join him in his office. As the head of Art and DT, he thought that Mr Thornhill should be properly introduced to his new sofa.

"Hmm – it's very well constructed, and a great improvement on the old one if you don't mind me saying so," commented Mr Thornhill. "Where did you buy it?"

"It was given to me by a pupil."

"Gosh, that was generous; it must have cost a packet."

"I don't think so. You see, it was made by Lara Frost."

Mr Thornhill was astounded.

"You mean that a Year 7 pupil made this?"

"Absolutely, and that is a talent I think we ought to nurture. Don't you agree?"

"Of course," replied his friend.

"Robert, are you feeling adventurous?" Mr Harris enquired with a wicked glint in his eye.

"Maybe," replied Mr Thornhill warily. The last time he had been adventurous with Marcus Harris, he had ended up travelling to France and back on a tandem.

DOI: 10.4324/9781003208044-14

"Have a seat." Mr Harris grinned, and Mr Thornhill gingerly sat on the sofa. "Ready?"

"For what?" Whoosh! There was a pause and then the sofa spluttered, "OK, I admit it. I wasn't ready for that!" Mr Harris pressed the button again, and Mr Thornhill reappeared, looking rather stunned.

"That is incredible," he said admiringly. "Can you do it again?" Whoosh – off he went.

Janice popped her head around the door.

"Lara is here to see you, Mr Harris." Lara arrived just in time to see Mr Thornhill appear out of the sofa, feet first, wearing a huge grin.

"Lara come in, come in," beckoned Mr Harris. "I was just showing Mr Thornhill your new invention."

"Lara, this is amazing. How did you get the seat to swing so smoothly in both directions?" Lara began explaining in detail how she had designed and improved the sofa until it was perfect. Mr Harris sat on the edge of his desk, delighted to see the pupil and teacher confidently discussing the technicalities of sofa design. Both of them were alight with enthusiasm and bursting with ideas.

Mr Thornhill eventually sat back on his heels, his face pink with excitement.

"Marcus, this is exceptional! I have never seen such a well-designed piece of furniture anywhere, let alone one made by a pupil. With your blessing, I would like to ask Lara to join the Designers Club."

"I thought you might," nodded Mr Harris.

Lara watched, feeling confused until Mr Thornhill explained.

"Lara, I run a DT club on a Thursday evening for a few of the most talented Year 12 and 13 students. We work on individual projects and also do a joint design project which is entered into *The Product Designers in Schools Award* each summer. Last year we reached the district finals. With your skills, you would be a great help on the team." Lara smiled slowly. She had never been asked to join a team before. Usually, she was not very good at working with other people. This was different. This would be working with people in a situation where she would be an expert, doing what she enjoyed most. She felt a glow of pride spread through her body. This was going to be fun!

Mr Thornhill and Lara left together, discussing the projects that he had planned for the Design Club the following week. He was still smiling about the sofa after Lara had returned to her lessons. He strode back towards the DT block, humming happily to himself.

He was just turning down a side corridor when an unexpected movement caught his eye. Break had ended five minutes ago and so the hallways were usually deserted at this time, but he spotted a movement near the Year 7 lockers. It was most likely a pupil collecting a book that had been forgotten, but for an unknown reason Mr Thornhill felt suspicious. He looked more carefully down the corridor and immediately recognised the back view of

Julia Smythe by the way she flicked her long blonde curls over her shoulder. She was intently concentrating on one of the Year 7 lockers. She was half turned away from him, so Mr Thornhill silently stalked down the corridor towards her. Julia appeared to be attempting to spray something through the vents at the top of one of the lockers. She was being careful to ensure that she used the spray at exactly the right angle but it was proving tricky. She was so focused on what she was doing that Mr Thornhill managed to approach her unnoticed until he was standing right behind her. Casually, he leaned against the lockers and cleared his throat. Julia Smythe jumped a foot in the air, dropping the spray that was in her hand. A flush of guilt spread up her throat to her newly dyed hairline.

"Blooming hell, Sir! What are you doing sneaking about the corridors in lesson time?"

"I was going to ask you the same thing," he replied coolly. They both stooped to pick up the dropped spray. To Julia's annoyance, Mr Thornhill moved more swiftly and swiped the spray from the floor before her fingers could reach it.

She scowled. "Give it back, Sir. It's mine. You've no right to take a girl's private possessions."

Mr Thornhill examined the small bottle in his hand. It appeared to be an old bottle of perfume, but the liquid inside the bottle was unusually dark. He rolled the bottle gently in his hand, while Julia shifted uncomfortably from one foot to the other. Next, he looked at the locker with which Julia had been battling. The nameplate clearly said *Lara Frost – Year 7.* Mr Thornhill stared directly into Julia's eyes. She swept her heavily mascaraed lashes up and down in a manner that was intended to be charming.

"Now tell me, Julia, why would you – a Year 9 pupil – be trying to spray perfume into Lara Frost's locker?"

"I thought it would be a lovely surprise for her, Sir," simpered Julia.

"Given that Lara can be very sensitive to sensations, I suspect that finding her books covered in your cheap perfume would be anything but a lovely surprise."

"Oh, it's not cheap, Sir. That stuff's £20 a bottle."

"Well, whatever the price, you shouldn't be inflicting it on other students. Follow me," he said briskly. Mr Thornhill marched back up the corridor with Julia swaying in his wake. He checked his watch. He really didn't have time to deal with this now. He should have been teaching his Year 12 class. He knocked on the door to Janice's office.

"Sorry to bother you, Janice, but I need to sort out an issue with Julia."

"If you're needing Mr Harris, I'm afraid he's gone home. He needed to rest," replied Janice.

"That's OK, Janice. I can deal with Julia myself. But could you keep an eye on her for a few minutes? I just need to phone through to the DT block to leave a message for my Year 12 class."

"Of course, Mr Thornhill; you can use the phone in Mr Harris's office."

"Thank you, Janice. Sit down, Julia. I'll be back to deal with you in a minute." He put the perfume bottle down on Janice's desk and went into the inner office. Julia slouched across two chairs and stared at Janice with a look of bored disgust.

Janice tried to continue typing the letter she had been working on, but Julia was very hard to ignore.

Eventually, Janice picked up the bottle on her desk and said brightly, "So what's all this about?"

"Just some perfume I brought in to give to a friend," Julia said silkily.

"Oh," said Janice. She put the bottle down and went back to her typing. Julia twirled her long golden curls around one of her fingers and continued staring at Janice.

"Miss, do you get all your clothes from a charity shop?"

"I'm sorry?" replied Janice, confused by the sudden turn in the conversation.

"It's just, I don't think I've ever seen an adult wear such an awful jumble of clothes. Even my nan has more style." Janice blinked and looked down at herself. She was wearing a cord skirt and one of her favourite woolly cardigans, which was almost the right shape. She was aware of a hole under the armpit, where she had dropped some stitches, distracted when her favourite TV policeman had been hanging off a building by one arm. She had taken to wearing her older clothes recently because her puppy climbed all over her as soon as she got home. Janice suddenly felt a little teary. It was hard being mocked by girls like Julia who were pretty and confident – attributes that Janice felt she had never possessed as a girl. She bit her lip and steadied her nerves.

"That is not a kind thing to say, Julia," she replied primly, hitting the print button on her computer harder than she intended. The printer on the other side of the office whirred into life. Janice smoothed down her skirt and rose with great dignity to cross the room and collect the printing.

She was only halfway across the small room when Julia shrieked, "O.M.G. I don't believe it! You're wearing odd shoes!" Julia whipped out her phone and began filming Janice's feet, narrating the footage as she recorded, "Look what the old bag in the office is wearing today! Look at her feet! She's come to school in odd shoes! The woman has no shame!"

Something inside Janice snapped.

"No shame!" she hissed back. "No shame! What would you know about shame!" Julia lowered her phone, slightly surprised to find that friendly old Janice actually had a temper.

"All right, deary, there's no need to get your knickers in a twist," said Julia mockingly.

"I'm wearing odd shoes because they're the only ones I've got," replied Janice with an icy edge to her voice.

"Well, buy yourself some new ones, you daft cow."

"I can't," spat Janice. "I can't afford to." Julia looked completely dumbfounded by the concept that an adult might not be able to afford to buy new shoes.

"Well, you're never going to get Mr Harris to fancy you looking like that," she retorted, flapping her eyelashes at Janice insolently.

"How dare you suggest that my relationship with Mr Harris is anything other than a professional friendship!" Janice had a sudden desire to pick Julia up by her perfectly styled hair and shake all the meanness out of her. Her eyes settled on the perfume bottle on her desk. She grabbed it, pointing the bottle at Julia. The girl immediately looked genuinely terrified.

"No!" she screamed.

"Perhaps it's time you took some of your own perfume!" Janice hissed, spraying three pumps from the bottle towards Julia's face. They both gasped. Then there was total silence.

"I think the usual metaphor is 'taking some of your own medicine'," commented Mr Thornhill from the door to the inner office, "which appears to be very apt in this situation."

Janice sank into her chair.

"Oh my days, Mr Thornhill! What have I done?"

Julia's face, torso and part of the display board behind her were splattered a deep, vivid blue.

"I think you have just accidentally covered Miss Smythe in blue ink," replied Mr Thornhill smoothly. "I thought that your 'perfume' was an unusual colour, Julia."

Julia sat frozen in time, the whites of her eyes staring crazily from her vibrant blue face. Very slowly, she lifted her speckled hands and looked down at her blotchy blouse.

"It really isn't a bad look, Julia," chuckled Mr Thornhill. "It would be very fashionable if you were a Pict from the fifth century. Never mind. It'll come off in the wash."

"It's permanent," murmured Julia.

"Oh, deary me. Well, even permanent ink comes off eventually, but it's going to take a bit of explaining to your parents. As is the fact that you were trying to spray permanent ink into the locker of a Year 7 pupil. I'll call them now and ask them to collect you."

Twenty minutes later, Mr Thornhill led Julia Smythe down the deserted corridor towards the car park where her mother was waiting. Their timing was unfortunate, because as they entered the main corridor, hundreds of students poured out of their classrooms. Most stopped dead when they saw Mr Thornhill escorting a blue phantom towards the exit. The strange thing was that from behind, the hideous spectre looked just like Julia Smythe.

A collective whisper swept through the crowd, "It's Julia Smythe." The words swirled around and around the corridor, mixing with sniggers and giggles, shouts and guffaws of laughter. These were soon followed by taunts.

"Hey, Julia, like what you've done with your make-up."

"I think you overdid the mascara, Julia."

"Blue is very fashionable this year!"

Mr Thornhill smoothly escorted her through the crowd.

"Right, off you go, everyone; there's nothing to see here. Julia just had a small accident with some ink that she brought into school."

As they neared the main exit, Julia broke into a run, pushing her way through the remaining pupils and out to the waiting car. To Mr Thornhill, she looked like a scorpion scuttling back to its nest, knowing that it had lost its sting.

Epilogue

Mr Harris sat on the immaculate cornflour-blue sofa that dominated his office. Above it was a large sign stating, *This sofa was designed and made by Lara Frost, who kindly donated it to the school.* It was a lovely place to sit at the end of the day. It was warmed by the passing sun, and he could see gaggles of students chatting and laughing as they left school for the afternoon. He was holding two envelopes in his hand.

It had been nearly two years since the accident. He flexed his fingers. No evidence was left of his broken arm, except for a small scar near his elbow, which he suspected would be an untroubling companion for the rest of his life. Both the envelopes in his hand had arrived that morning, and although they were not directly connected, they had both brought him great joy. Now, at the end of the school day, he had time to really indulge his pleasure. He reopened the first envelope and removed the thick cream paper. He began reading it again for the sheer joy of it, even though he already knew its contents.

Dear Mr Harris,

As you know, the judges have been considering the entries for The Product Designers in Schools Award. All the entries that reached the final of this year's competition were of an exceptionally high standard and all the pupils involved should be highly commended for their efforts.

 DOI: 10.4324/9781003208044-15

It is with great pleasure that I inform you that the team from Highfield Secondary School have been nominated as winners of this year's competition. So, my heartiest congratulations go to the four pupils involved: Sarah Bisset, Lara Frost, David Jones and Lakbir Singh. The judges were particularly impressed with their innovative furniture designs and the way in which the pupils worked together as a team.

I am delighted to award the school £5,000 to be spent within your Design and Technology Department and look forward to welcoming all four pupils on to our scholarship scheme in due course.

With my very best wishes,

Darren Johnson

Darren Johnson

Chairman

The Product Designers in Schools Award Committee

Mr Harris was so delighted with the outcome that he couldn't resist bouncing up and down on the sofa for a few moments. He had told Lara the good news in person when he had seen her with her friends by the vegetable garden. Her pleasure at her achievement was a wonder to see. He felt honoured to have played a small part in guiding her life towards that success.

She had said something surprising after he had told her the news. This in itself was not remarkable, because Lara often said surprising things. But her comment had stuck in his mind. She had said, 'Perhaps what people say is right. Perhaps school **is** the best time of your life.' It was an unusual comment, but then Lara was an unusual girl. He smiled and took a sip of his tea before turning to the second envelope.

Now this parcel really had been astonishing. Peeling open the end of the small package, he tipped the contents into his lap, then picked up and examined the little family of sheep. They were exquisitely carved from wood. There was a mother, a father and two lambs. All of them appeared to be grinning. Mr Harris pulled out the letter that accompanied them. It was from Mr Prendergast.

Dear Marcus,

I know I should have written to you many months ago, but embarrassment about my previous behaviour made me reluctant to contact you – cowardly of me, I know, but there it is. Fortunately, much can change with time. I wanted to thank you for prompting me to leave teaching at Highfield. It is clear to me now that I should never have trained to be a teacher. It seemed like the right thing to do when I left university, but I should have known that I am not well suited to working with young people. Being faced with the reality that I was an awful teacher and that the pupils hated my lessons made me angry and resentful.

When I left Highfield, I was furious with the world and for several weeks I sat at home blaming everyone else for my problems. Eventually, I decided that as there was no one I wanted to speak to, I would move far away from other people and live alone in Wales. I made this decision out of spite, thinking that everyone would be sorry when I left. But, of course, I doubt that many people noticed when I moved away and those who did were probably relieved to hear the news.

Anyway, I sold my house and bought a small cottage overlooking the sea. I acquired a stray dog for company and began to live my life by the rhythm of the tides and seasons. Over the months, I was befriended by an elderly neighbour who has spent his life restoring antique furniture. He has gradually taught me the skills of his trade and I realise that I have become his apprentice. I have increasingly taken over the running of the business under his guidance, leaving him free to retire. The solitary nature of the work suits me much better than teaching.

I found it was hard to stay angry when surrounded by the beauty of nature, and I have been slowly accepted into a thriving country community. As you once suggested to me, I have tried to notice positive things each day. I relish the sun in the morning, the feel of wet sand when walking on the beach and the warmth of the stove at night. A sense of calm and balance has returned to my life, which makes me realise how I had previously become consumed with bitterness and frustration. I must have been intolerable to work with and I am sorry for that.

When the anger began to recede, I felt like a new man. I have started to grow vegetables and now I keep sheep, chickens and a couple of cows on the fields that surround my cottage. I walk down to the sea each day with my five dogs - the stray I adopted surprised me by giving birth to four pups one night and she has proved to be a wonderful mother. I spend the evenings and rainy days creating wooden carvings, which sell well in the local markets. It is a simple life, but a happy one.

So, I wanted to write and say thank you, for pushing me towards a new path that has led to happiness. I hope that you will accept this family of sheep as a token of my gratitude. Perhaps Lara Frost should also take some credit because being trapped in her sofa was the catalyst that changed my life for the better.

I do hope that all is well in Highfield.

With best wishes,

Eric

Eric Prender-ghastly -I know that's what the children used to call me. I'm glad that now I find it funny!

"Well, well, well," Mr Harris murmured to himself. "Now, that is a letter that I never expected to receive."

Standing up, he went over to the window and carefully arranged his happy family of sheep on the window ledge.

Turning back, he glanced at the clock, aware that he really ought to get ready for tonight's parents' evening, then he looked fondly at the sofa.

"What the heck. Just once. It's such fun," the headteacher chuckled. He slid on to the sofa and, whoosh, disappeared under the seat.

A moment later, Janice knocked and entered his office. She was wearing a very smart pair of green shoes. They were a unique and elegant design, and when Janice took them off in the evening, a neat label was stitched inside saying: *Lara Frost Designs.* She glanced around the empty room and then stared accusingly at the sofa.

"Mr Harris, not again . . . Come out! . . . Mr Harris! I know you're in there," she called.

"Oh no I'm not," replied the sofa.